Short Stories by Archie

by
Archie Matthews

This book is a work of fiction. The characters, incidents, and dialog are drawn from the author's imagination and not to be construed as real. Any resemblance to actual events or persons, living or dead, is entirely coincidental. (The lawyers made me say that so as to protect the innocent……Me.)

Short Stories by Archie. Copy Right © 2014 by Archie M. Matthews. All right reserved. Printed in the United States of America. No part of this book may be used or reproduced in any manner whatsoever without written permission from the Author, except for in the case of brief quotations embodied in critical articles and reviews.

Books may be purchased for educational, business, or sales promotional use. For information please contact author by email at: archiemmatthews@gmail.com

To order a copy of this book, please contact; LuLu.com
ISBN 978-1-312-71352-9

DEDICATION

This Book is dedicated to my beloved wife Suzanne Matthews, Who has always listened to my stories and encouraged me through thick and thin.

All illustrations by my beloved and extremely talented wife Suzanne Matthews, an accomplished painter and illustrator in her own right, "Thank you for all your help!"

CONTENTS

The Monster Under the Bed	9
The Notorious Plastic Pliers	25
Pets in the Post	34
The Stink Eye	71
The Milk Jug Helmet	95
The Gunfight	105
The Dragline	119
The Hair Raising Yowl	157
The Henchman	183

Short Stories by Archie

The Monster Under the Bed

When I was about four years old I got a little plastic set of tools for Christmas. I distinctly remember the remark my father made when I unwrapped them. "Oh boy, here we go, that's all that kid needs to further destroy anything and everything we have of value… Thanks mom and dad." He said, a bit sarcastically to my grandparents.

At the time I was too young to recognize "sarcasm", but in the sixteen years of living with my parents, I became very experienced in recognizing it when I heard it. In fact, I got so good at recognizing sarcasm, that I could almost discern it from looks my dad gave me throughout my teenage years and even now into my adulthood.

Dear old dad is a "Skilled Sarcastic", even now. I'm fifty and he's close to seventy five, but I assure you his skills are still honed to a razors edge. Even now, as I sit writing this story, there he sits across the living room in his chair emanating "Sarcasm" as I type and read aloud bouncing my stories off him, my mother and my loving wife. Trust me, they are fantastic critiques. Each is utterly marvelous if you're into brutal honesty and wildly magnificent if you're into "cold hard facts", but enough of that, back to the story.

My Christmas tool set consisted of a hard plastic set of pliers, with a couple of screw drivers, a plastic saw and my personal favorite, the plastic hammer.

As any kid will do with a new toy, I immediately went right to playing with my small tool set. It didn't take me long to realize something was wrong. Of course being a "boy" I was immediately drawn to the "Hammer", but quickly realized, being plastic, the hammer wouldn't really pound anything. Try as I might to knock the arm off my mother's rocking chair, it just bounced off, much to the smiling satisfaction of all the adults, especially my sarcastic father.

I immediately realized I needed something softer than wood and my eye rested on our dog "Lady". Creeping up to poor old Lady Dog lying in her corner, one of her eyes opened as if realizing doom approached. This being one of my earlier experiments in life, I was able to get in one good whack to her noggin, but with the resulting growl from both Lady Dog and my mother, I quickly realized I'd better find something else to apply my hammer upon. Therefore I toddled off into the other room and began searching for my mother's cat.

Small children love to experiment on the household pets. Theologian psychologists might suggest it all stems back to the early "Bible Era" and the hard time Noah might have had with that ark full of animals and some kind of unfulfilled need for "revenge" against the beasts.

I and my mother's cat," Mr. Good Kitty", had a long running feud. Mr. Good Kitty had learned when wrapped packages arrived in our home, to seek a hiding place, for fresh implements of torture had arrived.

As usual, I had started with our old female black lab named "Lady Dog", and as usual she just lay there and took everything I dished out until my parents caught on and put a stop to it. So being a thinking, calculating human being, my past experiences, had taught me that Mr. Good Kitty would give me much more "Action" in the tormenting department. And since Mr. Good Kitty didn't feel the need to be subjected to my torture, until my parents came to her rescue she was much more animated during the chase…let alone the actual "capture and torture" process.

Oh, by the way, "Yes", I did say "She", for Mr. Good Kitty was a female. There had been some minor confusion on mother's part as to the actual gender of Mr. Good Kitty when she accepted her from a friend as a kitten. Mother had brought her home and immediately introduced her to me as "Mr. Good Kitty". Needless to say, it was several weeks before father realized the mistake and pointed out the discrepancy to my mother. By then it was easier to just live with the name than to try and teach me the difference between "Mr. and Mrs." Therefore, our female cat was forever called Mr. Good Kitty, much to the confusion of many an outsider.

Mr. Good Kitty had witnessed my arriving grandparents and immediately perceived the packages for what they were, "An arsenal of cat torturing devices"; and through the harsh conditioning liberally applied by this young boy, Mr. Good Kitty quickly understood she needed to beat a hasty retreat, which she did.

Archie Matthews

Being the young tot I was, I had no knowledge of the "Pavlovian Dog experiment", the theories on animal conditioning and/or learned responses. What I did perceive at my young age, was the cat caught on quick. Little did the cat know, but, I also caught on quick, and had been conditioned by my own experiences, as to where the cat usually hid to escape me. Quickly putting one and one together, even though I was still too young to understand addition, I quickly came up with the two hiding spots Mr. Good Kitty always ran to, and immediately set off to search them.

I first wandered into the laundry room and immediately noticed the hamper lid was closed and deduced the cat wasn't hiding there. The sight of the hamper started me giggling to myself as I remembered the "Cat and Hamper Incident". I instantly reminisced back to several weeks ago, when I, in "hot pursuit" had seen the cat's tail just as it disappeared over the edge of the hamper. Being the mischievous lad that I was, I had quickly shut the lid on "Mr. Good Kitty", and then wandered off to seek other mischief, instantly forgetting about Mr. Good Kitty and his captivity. Be it as it may, a couple of days later my mother had "unsuspectingly" opened the lid to set about doing some laundry. Loosed from her starving, thirsty and maddening confines, Mr. Good Kitty had instantly sprung out of the hamper in the search of food, water and someone to vent it's anger upon.

I giggled to myself remembering the screaming and excitement as Mr. Good Kitty leapt from that hamper. Somehow a couple days shut up in a hamper, with no food or water had given Mr. Good Kitty the newly acquired thirst of a trapped African lion. And as if that wasn't enough, it also endowed upon the sweet little feline, the physical aptitude of a starved Bengal tiger. Upon opening the hamper lid, both "Lion and Tiger" had suddenly been loosed upon my poor unsuspecting mother in the confined

The Monster Under the Bed

laundry room, it also decided to vent it's pent up anxiety on the only person available, dear sweet, unsuspecting mother.

I still recall the loud "yowls" and my mother's screams as clothes flew, just as I closed the door between me, mother and the vengeful Mr. Good Kitty. I giggled at the time, safely on the outside, while my mother and Mr. Good Kitty began rearranging the laundry room décor.

That evening as dad came home from work, dear mother met him at the door, with bedraggled expression and arm waving excitement, she described trying to fend off the vicious Mr. Good Kitty while she fought to open the closed laundry room door and escape. Ever attentive, dad kept shaking his head trying his best not to laugh as he listened to mother. Before too long, both were trying to work out several "theories" as to how Mr. Good Kitty had gotten there. All of which seemed to include me in some way, shape or form. But I do have to say, I had giggled to hear her declare, "We've Spawned a Monster". But dear old dad just smiled with kindness and replied with the phrase that would come back to haunt him for years to come, "Honey, he's only a boy....just a healthy active boy."

After discovering the closed hamper, I proceeded down the hall and into my parent's bedroom, my little plastic hammer swinging in anticipation of finding Mr. Good Kitty and experimenting upon her noggin. Past experiences usually found Mr. Good Kitty crouching in the far dark recesses of the closet, so it was there, that I concentrated my attack. Approaching, I noticed the sliding closet doors and saw one was in front of the other, dimly lighting the inside and calling for me to "Explore". I clearly remember the excitement of charging head on into the cavernous closet.

Archie Matthews

Every man reading this story will recognize the similarity between my dad's closet allotment and his own. As with every other married male in America, dad's allotment of closet space was a mere fraction of what my mother's portion was. Funny how it's always the woman that gets the heftier closet allotment. What I mean to say is it's funny until you stop and think about who assigns the space. In our home mother is and always has been the "Space Allotment Nazis", but the older I got, I came to realize all wives fall into this category. (Just don't tell my wife I said that.)

The closet door happened to be open to my dad's pitiful side of the closet. The first clue that it was my dad's side, other than its pitiful small width, was the huge open space beneath the hanging clothes. In our home, only a man's shirts are hung up, trousers are held in the dresser. Only later in life, did I also discover women horde dresser space, almost as much as they horde closet space. But that is an axe to grind another day. (I digress).

Although dad's shirts hung down, they still ended far above my head and I noticed the bottom of dad's side of the closet was piled high with mom's shoes. I was too small at the time to realize that when it comes to shoes, men don't even get a space allotment.

The bottom of the man's side of the closet is like a ravine at the base of a mountain prone to severe "Avalanche". It is covered by the overflow that has resulted from the huge pile of shoes the woman accumulates on her side. Dad's side of the closet was no exception to the rule and was about a foot deep with mom's shoes, (no pun intended.)

I slowly began to pick my way through the cavernous shoe pile and work my way towards the back. Every closet is a vast dark

The Monster Under the Bed

cavern to a small child, and though I was afraid of the dark, I did have my trusty hammer.

I remember feeling like the jungle explorer I had watched on TV. the night before. That fellow had a huge machete he swung back and forth, hewing grass, vines and jungle foliage out of his way as he cleared his path of travel. Even though I only had my plastic hammer, it seemed to be doing remarkably well, as I swung it to and fro. The result of which was my mother's long dangling dresses began swinging back and forth and dropping to the floor of the closet, clearing my path ahead, but piling up on my back trail.

As quickly as that jungle explorer had gone from one end of the tangled ravine to the other, I had just as quickly traversed from one side of the closet to the other, yet no Mr. Good Kitty in sight.

Then it struck me that my retreat back the way I had come, was now cut off by a huge pile of garments that had fallen victim to my swinging hammer. My only option was to press on....which I did.

Reaching the farthest end of the closet away from the opened door, I grabbed the first sliding door and with all my might, I slid it over to my dad's side with a bang. Immediately and quiet unexpectantly, I suddenly found myself in total darkness, what with both doors now being closed.

Being terrified of the dark, and then suddenly thrust into complete darkness, a cold bucket of fear was instantly tipped over my head as I was a washed in cold terror. After a brief moment of shock, I began clawing at the sliding door that now blocked my way to sunlight and salvation. But "alas" it was not to come easy, for my foot became entangled in a shoe, that my fear

Archie Matthews

crazed brain perceived as a demons' clutching paw, that's when my flimsy shackled terror broke loose.

If you've ever been a small terror filled child, you've surely experienced the mystery of how sounds get mixed up in the dark. I distinctly remember the demon's scream of satisfaction, or I imagine it was satisfaction, as it clutched my ankle.

When you're four, it's incredibly hard to discern between a demon's shout for glee and my own screams of terror. The one thing I'm sure of, suddenly there was a whole lot of noise at various pitches and decibel levels as I realized I was in utter darkness and "Clutched" around the ankle. The sound was deafening, or would have been if I had remained in there a half a milli-second longer.

When you're a kid shut in a dark closet, time takes on a whole different dimension, especially when you're terrified of the dark, and suddenly clutched around the ankle by a salivating demon. Even the minutest part of a split second seems like an eternity, when you're suddenly "clutched".

At the end of that milli-second and with the amazing superhuman strength that even Clark Kent would have envied; deftly using my plastic hammer handle, I pried the door open enough for me to squeeze through. I shot out of that crack like a bullet out of a rifle barrel and crashed into the side of my parent's bed, the demon claw still attached to my ankle.

Now I don't know if you've ever been clutched around the ankle by a demon's claw or not, but talk about "Rocket Fuel" to my young jet engine! I tell you what, my motor didn't even slow down as I encountered the looming edge of my folks mattress. I don't know if they have any kind of Olympic event like "Speed cliff climbing", but if they have, I'd now be sporting that gold medal.

The Monster Under the Bed

I was up and over that looming barrier so fast, that to this day I am surprised there wasn't a burned streak across the top of that quilt. Somewhere along the way, my death scramble to escape the deadly demon had shaken him loose and I fell to the floor on the other side, "demon clawless." Realizing I still had my life, let alone my foot, I was suddenly up and around the foot of the bed and exited my folk's bedroom, "Post Haste". (Meaning quicker than a cherry pit exiting uncle Tick's award winning lips at the County Fair's Seed Spit 'n Contest.)

Entering the hallway, after my narrow escape from the dark depths of the closet, I fell with my back to the hall wall panting trying to catch my breath.

After a few minutes, I slowly peeked through the doorway back at the closet that nearly became my tomb. I was just counting my blessings when Mr. Good Kitty bolted from under the bed I'd just scrambled over and came shooting out the door, over my lap and down the hall into my bedroom. The suddenness of his appearance up and over my lap, quickly robbed me of at least two of my nine lives.

It seems adrenaline lingers longer in small children fleeing from the dark as does the terror of having ones foot clutched by a demon, therefore I was still a bit jumpy. The only thing that saved me from an instant heart attack and sure death was it happened so fast, I didn't even have time to scream or pee my pants. And anything faster than a kid's bladder release mechanism is FAST!

After a few more minutes of once again catching my breath, the last explosive burst of adrenaline wore off and I felt the renewed vigor of excitement at seeing my elusive quarry dart into my bedroom.

Archie Matthews

"Ah ha," I whispered to myself, as I realized I had "Mr. Good Kitty" where I wanted him. For my bedroom was much like other little boys rooms. Many things entered, living or not, yet very few ever escaped.

I giggled at how close I was to my quarry. I chuckle again, even now nearly forty five years later to think about how naïve I was, in assuming I was the hunter and "Mr. Good Kitty" the victim. Little did I know, I was soon to come to the startling realization of who was truly "The Victim".

I slinked down the hall and through the open door, and eased it shut. "Ha, ha…..now I got you, Mr. Good Kitty", I thought, as my plastic hammer thumped into my open palm. My eyes scanned around the room, slowly searching every nook and cranny. I have to admit, my room was cluttered with toys, and there were many nooks and crannies. The remnants of "The Great War", still occupied most of the bedroom floor in a huge tangle of Tonka trucks, stuffed animals and a whole bag of plastic green army men strewn around the battle field.

I jumped to the front of my open toy box at the foot of my bed and raised my hammer ready to introduce Mr. Hammer to Mr. Good Kitty's think tank. But all that greeted me was a few green plastic army men that had subsequently missed "The Great War" and still lay resting in their barracks. I slowly put the lid down, thereby eliminating another hiding spot for Mr. Good Kitty. I then proceeded around the edge of the bed, up and over a pile of blankets that I had kicked off last night during yet another nightmare battling demons. The remaining smell of sweat filled terror still lingering upon the bed sheets; a stench of fear that only a child can smell and keeps smelling until nearly middle school. That is, unless he's lucky enough to get a night light for a birthday or Christmas present.

Nine out of ten psychologists surveyed will testify that a night light will shorten a kid's fear of the dark dramatically while enhancing his ability to stay awake during school lessons. (Authors note; now readers can't claim they've never learned anything useful, let alone a scientific fact from one of my short stories.)

Rolling over the heap of handmade quilts, I rolled under the bed as deftly as a Green Beret soldier into a "Vietcong's hidey hole". Landing flat on my belly my eyes taking a moment to adjust to the dim light, I suddenly realized just how close I was to utter "DOOM". Suddenly, my hair stood on end to think I now occupied the same space "The Monster Under the Bed" inhabited. My only comfort was it wasn't quite dark, but only a shadowy gloom beneath the bed.

I was just beginning to count my blessings at it not being impenetrable darkness, like the closet, when something caught my attention from the corner of my eye. My head slowly swiveled around and there in the far upper corner, in the deepest depths of shadow, I saw two gleaming yellow eyes glaring back at me.

It's a funny thing, how as a kid we don't stop to think about the consequences of our actions. What I mean is funny to some…..in this case, not so funny to me. Without a shadow of doubt, I suddenly faced the gleaming eyes of the "Monster Under The Bed". An icy bolt of lightning struck my backbone and I felt a quick chill down my spine.

Scientists might explain my hair immediately standing on end as static electricity from rolling over the cotton quilts and crawling along the carpet. But children are not so foolish. We understand and often experience "hair raising" in our terror filled nights

Archie Matthews

quivering in the dark, awaiting daylight, static electricity and be danged.

Somehow I had gone from a happy Christmas morning to the depths of despair accompanied by utter terror, now face to face with the monster that most people only catch fleeting glimpses of.

Sightings of "The Monster Under The Bed" are usually only glimpses of its hands as they shoot out and try and grasp a child's ankles as they jump into bed. As with most monsters, sightings are not the typically full eye to eye contact as I was now locked into.

I say "Locked into" because that's just what it was....I could no more break the yellow steel gaze that held me fast, than to have broken a one inch thick steel bar welded from my forehead to the monsters. Those yellow eyes held me frozen in the depths of time and terror.

Sweat immediately began to pool into every crevasse of my body and although I was keenly aware I held a hammer and potential weapon in my small mit; I was sadly aware that it was made of plastic, thus more useless than a feather against a charging rhinoceros. Or would have, if I had known what a rhinoceros was.

Eons passed, as I imagined worlds eroding and whole galaxies blackening and burning out, all in that split second, while I locked eyes with the "Monster Under The Bed". For it seemed like "Forever".

And slowly a strange feeling began to creep up and over me. For the first time in my life, I was experiencing my main spring winding up. It was my inexperience that kept me from realizing my salvation was slowly gaining momentum and about to burst forth. For up until that very moment, I had no idea of what a "Main Spring" was to a human being, let alone a terrified child.

Seconds ticked by as tension built up and adrenaline had swollen my veins to maximum capacity. Little did I understand it was but fuel, awaiting the spark to ignite within the coiled springs, we all call "muscles". And then as a far off distant siren slowly builds and announces an emergency vehicle rapidly approaching, I heard a low distant whine getting louder and louder.

There we were two souls locked into a struggle of "Devour or be devoured". The "Monster Under the Bed" facing the doom of utter starvation and obliteration. For it knew there would never again be such an opportunity to devour "this room's inhabitant".

Even a village idiot of a "Monsters Under the Bed", would recognize the severity of letting such a morsel escape. Such monsters lived, hoped and dreamed of one day having the quarry it hunted, so foolishly and freely offering itself as a willing sacrifice by crawling under his own bed. This particular monster knew to let me escape from its clutches now, would mean that I would never again dangle my juicy leg morsels, let alone those delicate toe digits within its reaches.

Never again would there be the remotest chance of latching onto this particular child's legs. These were the Monster's thoughts, I know, for it transmitted its intention to devour my very essence through those glaring yellow eyes. Its glare boring into me trying to congeal my blood to slow me down, so that it could easily catch me.

Suddenly the tension of my tight coiled mainspring had reached its limit and the latch that groaned within its bracket, could no

Archie Matthews

longer hold back the utter power it had held up to this very second. All hell broke loose, and with a screaming blast, the charged energy of two living souls both fighting for their very existence under that small bed burst forth.

My main spring cut loose and unwound with lightning speed and a resounding crack of thunder. Okay, ok, perhaps the crack was when my head hit the wood bottom of the box springs as I shot out from under the bed, the Monster hot on my trail. I will say, he's just lucky he never actually caught hold of me, for if he had he would have been drug to death before he could have fathomed a thought of letting go.

I shot from under that bed so fast, my plastic hammer was never to be seen again as it must have evaporated into nothingness as I hit "Mach nine" and broke the sound barrier at least a dozen times.

I quickly scrambled to my feet, revved my engine to maximum RPM's and shifted in high gear and "Popped the clutch" as I headed for the safety of mother far off in the living room.

But it was not to be, for I no more than gained my feet and was about to hit top speed of around a thousand miles per hour, when I came to an abrupt halt as a large strong hand clamped down on me from behind. There was a loud scream as all the air was sucked out of the room and the entire building started to implode. I instantly changed shape and became a tornado of flailing arms, legs, Tonka trucks and stuffed toys. The room filled with screaming plastic army men as the looming shadow with its humungous clutching hands held me as tight as my granddads blacksmith vise held soft pliable melting iron. I felt the heat of the center of the earth welling up and knew I was being dragged to the hot depths of Hell by the "Monster Under the Bed".

The Monster Under the Bed

Then, just as a taunt shoe string reaches its breaking point and expectantly "snaps", I succumbed to the clutches of the "Monster Under the Bed".

With no other option than to remain conscious and feel every bone crunched and sucked of it's marrow, I did what any other traumatized kid would do, I rolled my eyes to the back of my head and "Yup, the lights went out in Georgia!....except I was in Idaho."

The next thing I remember was floating in a sea of blackness and hearing a distant familiar voice calling my name….."Archie… Archie… Archie" the sweet voice called quietly to me, friendly, lovingly, calling to me from far above, and then a dim light became increasingly brighter and brighter until I slowly opened my eyes…..and looked upon heaven.

There stood my mother, leaning above me placing a cold cloth upon my forehead and calling my name. She had such a sweet welcoming smile that pushed back my cold black dread and an instant flood of relief over whelmed me. I became aware of the slow realization that I had somehow escaped utter death and doom within the steel grip of the "Monster Under the Bed."

I remember slowly smiling at the realization I was amidst my family in the well-lit living room. My head swiveled around and there sat my smiling grandmother and my burly grandfather the blacksmith. I then looked around to where my father should have been sitting in his easy chair, but was not.

And then I heard his voice calling down the hall to my mother, "Frieda!! Where's that iodine?" and down the hall tromped dad. He came limping into the room, looking as if he'd just crawled

Archie Matthews

from beneath a running lawn mower, over the rotors of a flying helicopter and run through a cement mixer.

 I'd saw chunks of severely masticated beef gristle in Lady Dogs food dish that looked "Good" in comparison to poor dad. And then a glimmer of realization suddenly dawned on me, that it must have been my dear old dad that had rescued me from the clutches of the "Monster Under the Bed". By the looks of him, he'd taken a lick 'n but had kept on tick 'n for there he stood. I smiled, with proud satisfaction; my dad had not only taken up the challenge, but had evidently soundly defeated the Monster that had pegged me for easy pickn's.

I was so proud; right up until dad spied me and asked with a bedraggled glare, "What the heck were you doing howling under your bed? And why on earth did you shoot out from under there like the devil was after you? And what in the world possessed you into clawing, scratching and flailing at me like some sort of demented crazy man? What on earth did you do to your mother's cat....it's still crouched under the bed hissing and won't come out!!! What are you some kind'a nut?!"

Although it was the first time I'd heard that last question, little did I know it wouldn't be the last. But it was the last time I worried about the "Monster Under the Bed"...nothing can quench the fact that my dad whooped him but good!!!

Dad's still got the scars to prove it. And I knew that monster would never be back to risk being whooped again. But of course, there was that Demon in the closet and his clutch......"oh dad.....?"

The Monster Under the Bed

The Notorious Plastic Pliers

Here I sit, fifty years old staring at my rugged, calloused hands and I wonder. I see the scars around the knuckles and back of my hands and rolling them over I notice the thick hard ridges that have mapped out all the wild places my hands have been and all the work they've done. Noticing how crooked my fingers are brings vivid memories flooding back to mind.

Did you ever put your finger where you absolutely, unequivocally knew it shouldn't go? I have and many times. What draws my fingers into those places is a complete mystery to me, even to this day.

I remember as a kid, I was always getting myself into trouble, but no particular part of my anatomy got me into more trouble than my fingers, save one. (But we won't go into that!) This is a wholesome family type book....or so my mother, wife and daughters are wroth to remind me. So back to the fingers.

My first harrowing instance of putting my finger where I shouldn't have was when I was four years old and received a small plastic tool set for Christmas. It was a small child's set of tools that included a plastic saw, a couple of screw drivers, a plastic hammer and the "Notorious Plastic Pliers", as they would later always be referred as. Even to this day, the mere mention of "The Notorious Plastic Pliers" set's my parent's nerves on end as well as my finger to throbbing.

My loving grandparents had arrived that Christmas holiday bearing all kinds of gifts and upon opening my tool set; I began trying my best to "tool" everything. I hammered the furniture with my small plastic hammer until I soon realized I couldn't destroy anything what with it just bouncing off, even my mother's glass coffee table top. I quickly tired of nothing being destroyed and soon took off after Mr. Good Kitty. But that's another story, let's just say, after recovering from that adventure, I turned my attention to one of the screw drivers.

I don't really remember which it was, the Phillips or the Regular tip, I just remember trying to "Screw and Un-screw" to my heart's content. Unfortunately for me, but quite fortunately for my parents the furniture and appliance owner's, they had nothing to worry about. That is until I tried to take the oven door off and touched the hot oven hinge with my plastic screwdriver tip.

The Notorious Plastic Pliers

Being Christmas day, my mother had been diligently cooking a turkey and ham in the oven since very early that morning. Therefore the oven and subsequently its door, both inside and out, were extremely hot. Upon touching the end of my plastic screwdriver to the hot oven door, it immediately stuck to the hot surface and being a kid, the effect was intriguing, therefore I continued to press the screwdriver into the surface as it melted to a nub. The plastic quickly boiled and then slowly turned from the bright orange it had been manufactured in, to a nasty dark brown color. That was about the same time it began to smell horribly.

As I stood there watching the brown glob slowly ooze down the hot stove door, pinching my nose with my fingers to stand the stench, the plastic suddenly hit ignition point and burst into flame. Realizing this was now and "Ought'O", I ran from the kitchen into the living room and announced the problem.

"Ought'o....Ought'O...." I shouted as I ran to the middle of the room, trying to get everyone's attention. But of course the adults were sitting engaged in deep conversation and didn't understand that something bad was cooking in the kitchen, and I didn't mean mom's Christmas turkey.

Making my third and final lap of the living room, and just getting patted on my head and ignored by each adult for my troubles, I quickly decided if it wasn't any big deal to the adults, it wasn't a big deal to me. Besides, I had another screw driver. So meandering back over to my Christmas plunder pile, I acquired the second screw driver and avoiding the stinking kitchen with its now "flaming oven door", I charged down the hallway and into the bathroom.

As everyone knows, besides the kitchen, no room attracts, nor enthralls a child like the bathroom. I was no different, but a

Archie Matthews

difference there was, for I had parents that stressed the fact that the bathroom was a "No, No" and punctuated the fact with punishment to my backside. But realizing the adults were in heated discussion in the living room, and beyond even caring about the flame engulfed oven door, I instinctively knew, there was no better time than "now", to explore the bathroom. I'd tried many times to explore those mysterious drawers in the bathroom, but had always been intercepted by either mom or dad. But now was my chance, and I seized the moment.

I had a thorough working knowledge that you could put things in the big white water fountain, pull the handle, and "Presto" an amazing water show began. Sometimes it went down, and yet other times, up it comes. Going down never really elicited the excitement from the adults as the "up it comes".

I had worked that silver handle many times in the past and was always amazed to see the down it goes, especially when a liberal wad of paper was shoved in while still on the roll holder. I had also learned a fellow only got a couple flushes and as many gleeful giggles, watching the paper spin and disappear off the roll down the water swirl, before an adult appeared. Therefore I knew there was a limit to my flushes before my backside was punished. Today I wasn't interested in the big white water fountain. Today I was more interested in the mysterious drawer by the sink.

I had watched my parents put in and take out all kinds of amazing things to and from that drawer, and today I was determined to explore it and its contents. I had watched dad install intricate latches that fit inside the drawer that my tender little fingers couldn't quite push to allow me to open that drawer. I had watched intently and knew that he had used a screw driver to install it. Being a little mimic and "Daddy's little man", I knew

The Notorious Plastic Pliers

by watching dear old dad, if a screw driver put it on, a screw driver could take it off. And here I was, screw driver in hand.

I worked that screw driver as deftly as any lock pick and after a few minutes of twisting and poking, I had that drawer just where I wanted it, "OPEN". My little hand went in and out removing everything and setting it on the floor. After a few moments, I had what I was most interested in, the toothpaste. Every morning and every night, my mother would brush my teeth. Of course she always controlled the mysterious tube of toothpaste, while I only got minor control of the brush. The thing that intrigued me the most was how she gently squeezed out a smidgeon of toothpaste, just enough to tantalize my taste buds, yet never enough to satisfy my hunger. But now I had the tube and I was licking my lips with anticipation.

I tried to work the "twisty top", but couldn't get it to open. I quickly realized I needed those "nifty grabbers" that dad used when trying to pinch things hard. The Pliers! Dropping the screwdriver I ran into the living room just in time to hear a commotion in the kitchen. The alarming shout from my mother instantly drew all the adults. I quickly realized my time was limited and grabbing my plastic pliers, I headed back to the bathroom and began working on the toothpaste "twisty top".

Who's to say just how it happened, after all, I was the only witness in the bathroom and I was only a child. But somehow my plastic pliers came disconnected and suddenly I held two pieces in my small hand. That's when another strange phenomenon happened and my finger made its way into that small hole that had connected the two pieces with a plastic rivet. Who can explain how a child's finger enters such a strange place? Perhaps I tried to reach through the small hole on my way to the toothpaste, whatever the case may be, in it went and past the second knuckle.

Archie Matthews

What I can explain, is my little finger easily slipped in, but when I tried to pull it out, it was suddenly locked fast. Nothing sets a little boy on edge as to suddenly realize a body part is stuck. I remember pulling and twisting just seemed to make it hurt worse and that's when I hit my panic button, which in turn set my siren off, as well as ignited the pistons to my running mechanism, and I was down the hall screaming my head off on my way to the kitchen.

I arrived in the kitchen just as the adults had doused my flaming screw driver remnants on the side of the hot oven door. Yet before they had actually figured out what the now blackened gob was. Immediately I ran to my mother who doubled as my own personal physician and quickly began screaming "Owie, Owie, OWIE"! All the while running in a circle waving my blackening finger with one half a pair of plastic pliers still attached.

As I made the third lap around the small kitchen, my siren at its maximum volume, dear mother bent down and scooped me up. I of course was quick to thrust the throbbing finger complete with attached plastic pliers as close to her face as possible and once again inform here as to my discomfort and screamed, "OWIE!" She quickly assessed the situation and gave a raised eyebrow look at my now blue black finger stuck through the hole of one side of my plastic pliers.

"Oh my goodness, what's this?" she asked.

My dad stepped up close and seeing what was going on, tried to do the manly thing and began trying to tug and twist my finger off. He might have just cranked up the "Volume" dial on a stereo, for my screaming instantly became louder.

And then dear old grandpa stepped close and with a smile he said, "Give me a sharp kitchen knife and we'll cut it off".

The Notorious Plastic Pliers

With that being said, the resulting explosion of instant pandemonium at the realization they were going to "Saw off my finger with a kitchen knife", ensued. After several moments of uncontrolled thrashing and clawing trying to escape, I was subdued beneath one arm of my eight hundred pound father "the gorilla", his other arm had my hand locked firmly, while my blood thirsty finger sawing grandfather approached holding the enormous butcher knife.

Seeing my digits impending doom, I struggled as any creature would that recognizes the dark cloaked figure of death and destruction slowly approaching, but it was fruitless. I might have been held fast on the outside, but I let them know my lungs with screaming mechanism still attached were still under my direct control. Therefore I counter attacked and sought to fend off my assailants with my "tonsils of vengeance". They might saw off my blackening finger, and I might be doomed to live with only nine fingers. But they would certainly pay with any hearing they now had. It was with that solemn oath to myself, that I cranked my volume to the maximum.

Screwing my eyes tightly shut, for I didn't want to experience both the pain and visual trauma, I sucked in another huge lung full of air and "slice" it was over.

I remember thinking "Wow, that didn't hurt....in fact it even felt better." And I opened my eyes to see my finger slowly gaining its color back and my dear old grandpa holding what remained of the "Notorious Plastic Pliers".

There was a mild celebration as the adults congratulated one another on a job well done, that or they were just thankful my screaming had stopped. And after a brief examination and satisfied my finger was taking on a more natural hue, dad sat me down on my feet.

Archie Matthews

Brief the celebration was, for an angry shout suddenly burst from down the hallway coming from the bathroom and I realized mother had found the jimmied bathroom drawer, not to mention its contents strewn about the room. It's kind of funny how contents so neatly arranged, can get "Strewn", when one's finger is suddenly threatened and turning black.

I was trying to decide if it would do me any good to seek the safety of my grandmother's side, when I heard the sweet old woman declare, "If I didn't know better, I'd say that was the smell of burning plastic coming from the stove." My mouth instantly dropped open and I remember standing there awestruck that my own kind grandmother had just ratted me out.

Dad and granddads' head's began to swivel back and forth from me to the stove and the blackened spot of screw driver….not to mention I could hear my mother coming down the hall…..and if you've ever heard "impending doom" approaching you'll know just what it sounded like. To this day, my backside quivers when I see lightning and hear the rolling rumbling of thunder approaching.

I'd like to say, that I grew out of that habit of sticking my fingers and other digits where they had no place being put. I'd like to say that, but I can't.

It seems quite apparent to me that fingers were designed and meant to be "Poked into places". I've used my fingers to test all kinds of things, from electrical sockets, to spark plug connections. My fingers have dug out belly lint and ear wax as well as other noxious matter that I won't go into detail here about.

32

The Notorious Plastic Pliers

My fingers have been used as indicators, such as pointing in which direction I was about to go, as well as suggest to others which direction they should go, sometimes as an act of kindness and at other times not so friendly , but enough said about that as well.

These digits of mine have suffered a great deal over the years, for although I only have ten fingers, I have broken a total of twelve…..so far. I have all but detached a couple, having just hung by a thread until expertly reattached by emergency room technicians by more thread. Yet, I've never broken my "Lucky Thumb"…..yet.

I would like to say that the "Notorious Plastic Pliers" was the first and the last thing to have to be cut from around one of my fingers, but as I've said before, I can't. More than once while working as first a Cabinet Maker and then as a Carpenter, my bosses where aggrieved to have to destroy parts of equipment and/or other various construction projects, to free me and my finger/s. Many was the time a job superintendent handed me a long screw driver or spud wrench and explained "THAT is to be used to stick into places….NOT YOUR FINGER!"…usually it was upon my return from the local hospital with a broken finger or two in a fresh splint.

The past several years my beloved wife has assumed responsibility for me and continually tries her best to help me avoid "digit driven emergency room visits". I have to admit the woman has succeeded "by far" where others were complete failures. But even now that I am fifty plus years old and know better, without even thinking, my finger will instinctively go where it shouldn't.

My wife suggests "this is where I should put a moral to the story," so here goes.

Archie Matthews

"Guys…..don't put your digits where they don't belong. We wouldn't have the problems that we have in the world, if Adam had kept his digit to himself, but he evidently didn't and therefore the gene was passed down from one guy to the other and the direct result is with us today."

"Are we still talking fingers?"

Pets in the Post

Did you ever reach into a hole or perhaps some other cubby and get the surprise of your life? Well I did many years ago as a small child and the horror has stuck with me all these years. Here's my story of that long ago day.

Once again I had been set free from the local child holding facility known as the Grandview Elementary School. And as in years past, seeking a refuge of peace and solace for at least the summer vacation months, I went to spend the summer with my beloved grandparents in Ola, Idaho.

Just how old I was at the time is still a topic of heated debate between I and my dad as he sits in his chair in the corner of our living room. Dad's seventy five now and claims his mind is clear as a bell, well I would agree, except for this particular argument.

Dad is adamant that was the same year his parents, my grandparents, had gotten their evil little dog "Festus", but since there is no mention of him anywhere in this story, I contend that my dear old dad is "miss remembering", which, as everyone knows, is what happens when your seventy five. It's about here in our argument that dad gets really heated up, which is also a trait when you reach seventy five and are corrected by your fifty year old son. I am the one he often refers to as "Mr. Wisenheimer".

Be that as it may, what precise age I was really makes no difference unless you're apparently a seventy year old codger with a "Mr. Wisenheimer as a son!" Therefore I will refrain from mentioning just precisely what age I was, in order to hopefully pacify the seventy five year old grouch living in my home, along with his seventy five year accumulation of hunting rifles, complete with ammunition. Need I say more?

That year we had experienced a very cool spring, and summer had come a bit later, therefore all the little critters had tried their best to defy Mother Nature by waiting to have their young until warmer weather. I remember that well for grandpa made several remarks that year, at how late the song birds were hatching. This was also the year that grandpa brought home the "Strange looking puppies".

My grandpa Matthews was the town's blacksmith and a kinder gentler man was never to be found. Grandpa, although a hunter and fisherman, held a remarkable respect for wildlife, especially baby wildlife. He was the one that had championed a mother skunk that had given birth to several babies under the back porch of the general store the summer before, firmly fending off any and all ideas the town folk, especially Ed Shotz the store owner, had about "rooting them out and getting rid of the lot!"

The Pets in the Post

Grandpa had argued "Each and every critter has a God given right to have a home, and if not a permanent home, at the very least a safe place to birth it's young and raise them". He even went on to ask, "How would everyone feel if their children were born and then were smoked out and run off without a place to raise them in?" The man had been fortunate enough to have had three healthy children and raised each of them in the same home he'd occupied until his death.

Now don't get grandpa wrong, he wasn't a tree hugger or a nut when it came to wildlife. He was the first one to say, "God put animals on this earth for man to benefit from, be that a smile, to pull a plow, to ride or to eat." But he was also compassionate and angered quickly if he saw anyone abusing one of God's creatures. He taught all us boys to hunt and to fish and to respect what we killed by giving "Thanks" and consuming our meat. We never hunted for trophies nor did we ever mistreat our livestock, it just wasn't done.

To say grandpa was attuned to Nature was to say the least, the man paid attention to the woods that surrounded the little town of Ola, and he paid even closer attention to its inhabitants. I've seen my kind grandfather pass up cutting a standing old snag that would have made wonderful firewood right beside the road ready and easy to load. But one look at the nearby stream and the woodpecker hole in the water facing side, told grandpa there would be a family of wood ducks either inside or on their way, and that tree was passed up without a second thought.

I also watched him once, so many years ago, catch a magnificent steelhead in the North fork of the Salmon River and after several minutes of careful scrutiny, he released the fish unharmed. When I huffed and puffed with astonishment at seeing him release the biggest fish I'd ever imagined, he just smiled and said, "My boy that was a hen and full of eggs. If we'd taken her and eaten her, we'd have a fish for one meal. But in turning her loose, we'll soon have hundreds if not thousands for

Archie Matthews

many a meal to come." I still remember his twinkling eyes and his smile as he enjoyed the wildlife for the blessing it was.

So that summer when grandpa had gone up to Uncle Tick's and done some "horse trading", even though he came back without a horse, it didn't surprise me or grandma he had come back with a pair of wildlife orphans. Grandpa had them in a burlap sack and had brought them from the car to the front porch, the bag whining all the way. I and grandma were about fit to bust with curiosity, I being curious and grandma about fit to bust, for she was not as fond of wayward critters as grandpa or I.

As kind and considerate of little critters as my grandpa was, grandma wasn't, or should I say she just had a harder time realizing the long term benefits of keeping wild critters at their house. And if you knew grandpa you'd know the man was a one man critter orphanage, or so it seemed most summers. He'd raised a couple of raccoons one year and grandma said "Those egg sucking, butter stealing rascals were about the death of me." And she'd meant it. Those coons had set the house on fire twice and only by the grace of God and grandpa being fast with a fire extinguisher, had major catastrophe been averted both times. For both times grandma had been trapped upstairs and would have gone up in flames had the house been consumed. Thus, ever since the "coon years", grandma had very little appreciation for "Wayward waifs of the wild life persuasion".

Upon entering the porch, grandpa was greeted with two totally different opinions, I on the one hand was smiling from ear to ear with anticipation, while grandma on the other hand, was frowning from ear to ear for the want of a good antacid. Grandpa being the smart old bear he was, quickly opened the bag and produced two little pups.

And then as lengthy and detailed a "Windy" as I have ever known my grandfather to tell, come whistling out of the pines. In reflection now, I am sure that is where my story telling ability comes from, although my grandmother was fond of saying her side of the family was related to Samuel Clemens. This was the first and to my recollection the only time I can ever remember grandpa telling an "untruth". As we would later find out, for puppies grow and as happens with many things, they grow into something entirely different than they originated as.

The "puppies" granddad had explained had been born to a German Sheppard female that didn't make it through the birth and because she had been so mistreated and starved, she had not only died, but had only these two "wee waifs". Since everyone knew how grandpa had pledged to right all wrongs perpetrated upon the animal kingdom at the hands of selfish evil masters, grandma could only nod and stomp off. Grandpa had quickly let his "woe betide us if we don't have pity, "expression fade from his face as grandma had exited, and gave me a quick wink and a smile.

Thus began the "Summer of the strange puppies" as dad still recalls it, but although the puppies were a large part of this summer and hold a role in this story, they were not the "Pets in the Post", for which this story is all about. But we're coming to that, now that we've come almost around the bush.

Grandpa had deposited the tiny puppies with me and extracted an oath to keep them under constant guard and ever a watchful eye, for as he explained, they were small helpless creatures and grandpa was worried about his big old Tom cat "Bob" getting wind of them.

Now old "Bob" was a huge black and white bobbed tail Tom cat grandpa had owned longer than he'd had me. Bob was a "fantastic mouser" or so grandma was often singing his praises as we would frequently see him cross the yard with the tail of his last meal still protruding from his mouth, be it a mouse or bird.

But as much as grandpa duly appreciated and loved his cat, he was never want to ignore the creatures "God given nature". Grandpa often said, "That cat's a killer, ever little furry or winged creature better watch out when old Bob is hungry and on the prowl". As I had seen Bob catch and devour many a large and

Archie Matthews

small bird, as well as mice, gophers, chipmunks and even large red squirrels when he could, I knew that was no small boast.

So I stood a watchful eye over those two little whimpering fuzz balls as grandpa went out the gate, over to the general store and soon returned with a brown paper bag and a frosty bottle of pop in his hand. Although I had a good idea who the soda pop was for and smiled and licked my lips, I hadn't a clue what was in that paper sack and couldn't hardly contain myself as I followed grandpa in the house.

Grandpa had picked up the puppy bundle, gone right in the kitchen and I had been left with that bottle of pop and the "you stay here smile". Now separated by the double swinging door and from the heated conversation in the kitchen that now ensued, I'd learned the hard way of the dangers of trying to listen with my ear up against a door that swings out, just as quickly as it does in, and thus I took myself around to the back porch. Experience had taught me that if a fellow was careful, a young lad might catch a break and the little kitchen window might be open to make eaves dropping possible.

I could hear grandma giving grandpa "What for", as in "What for are we going to do with these two pups when they grow up into dogs?" As well as hearing grandpa giving as good a "what for" as he got by replying, "What for? Clara, how could we abandon these small creatures to a fate of death before they ever experience life?" I knew just the heart melting look he was so liberally applying. I'd seen that look with half a dozen chipmunk pups, the two coon babies, a couple of crows with broken wings and a magpie, not to mention all the other countless critters. Like I said, grandpa was a champion for wildlife and everyone knew it. Many was the time people would bring this or that critter to my granddad's blacksmith shop for tending and mending, or just to be left "anonymously" in a box to be found the next morning.

I never did understand how grandma could argue with that, but of course I hadn't had any experience with women, let alone a

The Pets in the Post

wife. I'd better stop there so I don't get my married self into trouble, I suspect I am on the verge of a dire drop off if I venture further, therefore I'll change the subject back to the story. But before I go, I will risk saying, grandpa somehow had what still eludes me, even after all these years of being married, for he quite often got his way. Which in my case, I am still waiting for. The man was a reasoning magician when it came to talking to his wife. Many has been the time I've wished I had the man's tongue, for I never could make those kinds of miracles happen, with my own. But enough of that, we still have a ways to go around this bush.....Back to the story.

So after a long quiet session and then some banging pots and pans, I heard the door to the firebox on the kitchen stove open and wood being shoved in and knew something was "a cook 'n". I was also hoping the banging pots and pans hadn't been over grandpa's head and grandma wasn't now disposing of the evidence in the firebox. But after a few minutes out came grandpa with the pups under one arm and a bowl of warm milk. I sat quietly, still astounded grandpa was unbattered, let alone physically able to feed a bowl of milk to puppies. I was quick to notice the small "eye dropper" that grandpa began sucking milk into and holding it to the wee puppy's mouths, slowly feeding the little wigglers until their bellies stretched tight as drums.

For the next three weeks or so grandpa hand fed the puppies until they were soon wobbling around on their little feet lapping up milk from a bowl placed in front of them. It wasn't until several more weeks passed that we started to notice odd things about those puppies, but that's later in the story...for as you're probably catching on to, I tend to beat around the bush, and we got a ways to go yet before we get to the other side.

Then one fine day I was out in the back yard when I noticed a large red breasted Robin fly from the huge Russian Olive tree down to the top of one of the big round posts that comprised the cross arm for grandma's clothes line. Back then, most people owned electric driers although most still had clothes lines to hang

Archie Matthews

wet clothes on in the fresh outside air. Since grandpa and grandma's place didn't have power yet, they were still without the modern convenience, therefore they used the clothes line quite frequently.

The clothes line consisted of two large round posts set deep into the ground many years ago by grandpa and his father. Close to the top, but a good two feet shy of the top was a large wooden cross beam, that had been hand hewn into a square timber and mortised to snuggly fit the post. The cross bean was then bolted with several handmade bolts heated and headed upon the forge and anvil and then threaded with a die and a tapped nut to fasten nut to the bolt. This was how things were constructed by a blacksmith with loving care and build to last through the years, and it had.

What stood out to me as I noticed that large Robin fly from tree to post, was it hadn't just set upon the top of the post like it should have, but had disappeared into the top. I walked around and around looking at that post trying my best to see what the heck was going on. I'd seen trees with woodpecker holes in the side that made for many an entrance for squirrel or bird, but never seen a bird disappear like that. And being a kid my curiosity had been fired up and I was suddenly on a mission to find out what the heck was going on.

Being young though I was, I was still old enough not to be a conspicuous moron and draw the immediate attention of every nosy adult in the county by trying to fetch a ladder in the full light of day. Nothing fired up the suspicion in adults like a kid with a ladder, and since I was terrified to death of the dark and being devoured by ghouls and demons and such, I certainly wasn't going to try it in the dark either. That was when I began to set my mind on the puzzle of how to climb a pole without a ladder and being caught by my naturally suspicious grandmother.

"Why" you might ask, "Would you not want your loving grandmother to see you climbing her clothes line?" Looking back now, I can't fathom what my young mind had conjured as a

"Reason" to my madness. Being a grandpa now, if my young grandson came to me and said he wanted to look atop a pole where a bird had disappeared, I'd be hard pressed to keep from stampeding over the curious lad, for the want of satisfying my own curiosity, let alone his. But this is now and that was back then. What a young boy reasons inside his own mind at that age has been lost to me long ago.....okay, maybe I remember a smidgeon.

I doubt it was any single one of the thousand and one things I'd done and gotten in trouble for that had instilled inside me the need to keep my adventures secret from adults. For it seemed back then and even now, that almost every adventure I ever had, ended with me and an adult in the woodshed. And I'm not talking about fetching wood or coal for the stove, either. I had learned many a lesson at the business end of my dad's belt and my grandmother's willow switch in grandma's woodshed, amongst others.

I don't know if you've ever experienced a master torturer wield either a belt or a willow switch, but believe me when I tell you, it is an experience best avoided. Therefore I avoided it at every opportunity and "Yes", usually I got it in the end, but just like taking medicine, we each try to avoid it until they grab our nose and push the spoon in our mouths. And with that said, I began to quietly assess how a pole might be climbed as quickly and efficiently as possible without detection. My hope was to get up and down without spooking either bird or adult in the process. And as you will eventually read, I did one to great success, while the other I failed miserably at.

After many a day of deep thought and upon seeing that Robin on many more occasions fly down and disappear into the top of that clothes line post, I finally came up with a way to scale the clothes line. For one morning while setting out some food just inside the woodshed for "Bob" the old tom cat, I found an old rickety wooden chair with a half rotten cane seat just to one side of the door.

Archie Matthews

I vaguely remembered that chair had once set out on the front porch until my large aunt Edna had sat in it a couple years ago and it had bucked her off and onto the floor. Of course grandma, Edna's sister quickly pronounced the whole episode the chair's fault, of course later I heard grandpa suggest it might have been Edna's size. Either way, the chair had disappeared and grandpa had been chastised with an ugly look from grandma for even mentioning Edna's size.
But now the mystery of the missing chair had been solved and I was determined to use it to solve the "disappearing Robin" mystery.

As with most kids, my life was just one "Mystery" after another. I was still trying to unravel the great mystery of where the heck the Easter Bunny spent his time the other 364 days of the year before and after Easter. I also spent many a Christmas Eve trying to stay awake and catch old Saint Nick coming down our wood stove pipe. That's a mystery I tried for years to solve but never did. It seems the fat old rascal had a snitch in our house that let him know when I was still awake. Or at least that was my final opinion on the matter since he always came right after I'd fallen asleep even while deep undercover.

Once again, we got a ways to go around the bush till we get to the end of the story.....so onward!

I had waited until grandpa had left that morning for the blacksmith shop and grandma had been pushing her little mechanical sweeper duster around. Seeing the adults preoccupied with their chores, I quickly made my way to the wood shed and opening up the door, I carefully peered inside. As I have mentioned before, as a child I was deathly afraid of the dark and the woodshed having no windows was a great harbinger of darkness. Even with the door wide open, deep and lingering shadows threatened to conceal many a deadly end for a young boy, should he venture within "Clutching" distance.

 As every kid knows, sunlight is every monster and/or Demons bane, but a dark shadow can conceal a monster until an

The Pets in the Post

opportunity presents itself with an unsuspecting passerby and out shoots the monsters claw or tentacle and the child is "Clutched" and drug into the shadowy depths to be devoured. I had up to date, made it a lifelong pursuit not only to remain "unclutched" but also "undevoured" and therefore was extremely cautious of shadows and their lurking inhabitants.

After several minutes of peering deep within each and every shadow in the woodshed, calculating the odds and lengths possible to allow "Clutches"…… I quickly dodged over the threshold and back again, feigning entry only to dodge back outside again, all the while keeping close eye on each and every dark patch within. After doing this a couple more times and seeing no sign of tentacles or claws, I once again dodged inside the door and grabbed the chair then quickly hustled it outside. Getting the chair clear of the door, I quickly shut the Demon's lair with a bang and wiped the beaded sweat from my fear soaked brow. "Whew", another "darkness encounter" survived, I quickly congratulated myself and proceeded onward.

Dragging the chair over to the clothes line post, I quickly climbed up and standing precariously astride the caned center of the chair, I was astonished to find I was still far from my goal of actually looking inside the top of the post. Disappointed, I realized I could only barely reach up to the top of the post. Therefore stretching to my fullest height and reaching over the top of the post, I felt around. I was a bit surprised to find quite a depression and standing up on my very tip toes was able to feel a bowl like depression and there inside, were two small round objects. Gently taking hold of one, I pulled my hand back over the top and bringing my hand close to my face, I realized I now held a small blue egg. So this was where the Robin was disappearing too, a nest containing two small blue eggs. I smiled at my discovery and then hearing the Robin scolding me from the nearby tree limb, I quickly put the egg back and scampered back down the chair.

I must say the rest of the day I swaggered around pretty proud of myself for not only my ingenuity of discovering the chair, but my

Archie Matthews

bravery in pulling it from the dark den full of shadowed "Clutches; not to mention I had also solved the "Clothes line mystery". Of course it would have been ten times better if I'd had someone to share the entire adventure with, but I didn't dare let either grandma or grandpa into the fold, for fear of adult reprisals. It's one thing to brave being clutched by a monster and drug to a bloody death, but it's far worse to be clutched by an adult and drug inside to face the end of a belt or willow switch for "molesting wildlife". (For if the truth be told, I'd never actually seen a monster, let alone been clutched, while on the other hand, I'd been switched many a time before and knew full well the hard cold realities of getting caught.)

I'd never really been clear on the "Molesting" part, but grandpa assured me when I was "bothering critters", it's called "Molesting". Which in my teen years, had also been the term used by my girlfriend's angry father one evening as we were parked up by the reservoir and he happened along when he had. It seems we had all come up to the lake for some late night fishing, although each of us had been in hopes of catching something entirely different than we actually had. Funny how one word can mean all kinds of things....one time it can mean "bothering critters" and the next it can mean, "Murder" if your caught smooching my daughter again, or so her dad assured me. But once again, I am straying off the plot of the story at hand.

As with most summer vacations the days quickly came and went and before I even knew it half the summer was over. Several things had slowly and inexorably taken place over that period of time; the "puppies" had grown considerably and I began to see the Robin come and go with night crawlers and grasshoppers held in her beak to and fro visiting her nest. It wasn't to long before I began to hear chirping and realizing the eggs had hatched, I began to think another visit to the top of the clothes line was in order.

Meanwhile, the puppies had grown quite a bit and were starting to exhibit strange behavior for German Sheppard's and I wasn't

The Pets in the Post

the only one that thought so. The "pups" as we called them, had begun showing odd behavior. It didn't take a rocket scientist to realize they were by no means lap dogs. They despised being caught and held and would nip with their little sharp teeth, therefore I gave them quit a wide berth. The other strange thing was, they stalked the shadows and kept to the edge of the yard and foliage. They skulked around and would hide in the flower beds and under the massive trumpet vine that surrounded part of the front yard, all down the side yard, over a trellis that went up and over a gate and down the other side, ending around the far corner and to the edge of the woodshed. The pups would peer out of bushes and never frolicked or played like other puppies. Several people had made remarks about the pup's strange sneaky behavior and grandpa would always avoid the topic one way or another and change the subject.

Then the day came when Uncle Tick and Aunt Edna came to visit with their daughter, Cousin Trish. Trish was a beauty and as sweet a girl as there ever was and because she had always been kind and considerate to me, I had little trepidation in learning she was going to stay a couple weeks with us. (The little trepidation, meaning I'd have had a fit, if I'd had any choice in the matter, but didn't, therefore the "little trepidation".)

 It seems Uncle Tick and Edna were going to visit Uncle Tick's relative in Colorado, in what grandma had referred to "As the Big House". It was a long drive and was expected to take the better part of a week there and back, Uncle Tick had explained.

Grandpa's opinion was they'd never make it in their old car and joked that we'd probably never see them again. "But we'll do our best to raise up Trish the best we can." He'd chuckled. He and Trish had been the only ones smiling at the time, Tick and Edna had both tried to ignore grandpa's gloomy prediction and had just kept on rattling to grandma what they were going to do on the way to and from "The Big House".

After a long afternoon of visiting about everything under the sun, (Mostly Aunt Edna complaining about everything under the sun,

Archie Matthews

all the while Uncle Tick nodding and looking hang dog sad.), soon Uncle Tick and Aunt Edna both said their "Good byes" and after giving Trish a kiss goodbye, off they went in their old smoky car.

After dinner that evening I immediately set off towards the outhouse to "Water my Mule". Of course Trish being a girl, she was expected to wait and come along after I had gotten back, and then she would go and "Visit the water closet". Of course it's all very confusing when you're a kid, since we had no mules and there wasn't water in the outhouse, let alone in a closet.

But I headed out the back door and was off to the outhouse while the sun was still up, so that I didn't have to run the gauntlet of "kid devouring monsters" with my flashlight. And then I realized as I approached the clothesline and was about to make the turn out the side gate, now would be a fantastic time to visit the clothesline pole where I had heard the chirps of baby birds coming from.

After once again braving the woodshed and dragging the old rickety cane bottom chair outside and to the clothesline pole, I quickly scrambled up and thrust my hand up and into the open topped post. Feeling a squirming little chick, I quickly brought him back down for a look.

The little bird had some feathers, but was still mostly bright pink hide, with a big belly and little bright yellow beak with what appeared like huge lips on each side. I've got to say, it was an ugly little thing that chirped and wiggled around with its gaping mouth held wide open and straight up into the air waiting for something to be dropped inside. After several seconds of turning the little fellow this way and that, I stretched back up on my tip toes and reaching up, placed the noise maker back into his nest. Sure enough I could feel the other baby bird wiggling around and instantly knew both eggs had hatched.

After dragging the chair back into the woodshed, I then continued through the gate and down the path to the outhouse.

The Pets in the Post

After having "watered my mule", coming back up the path and in through the gate, I was surprised to see the puppies playing tug of war with something just to the side of the back door. Thus, as every kid would, I quickly went to investigate and discovered they had what appeared to be the remains of a red squirrel. They were each growling and pulling trying their best to out-do the other and run off with the whole thing, but neither could quite shake the other, so around and around they went, growling and tugging. As I approached one dropped his end and both scampered over to disappear underneath the trumpet vine, squirrel and all.

I went in through the back door into the still empty house and therefore went out the front door to the front porch. Everyone was sitting there on the front porch, grandma was rolling a ball of yarn while Trish had both her hands up holding a large fold of yarn looped over each hand letting the yarn loop off and onto grandma's ever growing ball. Grandpa sat in his chair, tinkering with a crank operated hand held can opener that he'd bought the last time they were in town. Grandpa had always been fascinated with any and all mechanical contrivances and as grandma was often heard remarking, "The man would buy a better mouse trap ever day of his life if they could make them fast enough."

Seeing me back from my "Mule Watering Expedition", Trish excused herself and took her own trip out to the "Water Closet", while I broached the subject about the pups with grandpa. "How come those pups are so stand offish? They sure aren't friendly like other puppies." I remarked looking at grandpa.

"Animals is each different." He answered still fiddling with the can opener and never looking up.

"And how come they always skulk around, they give me the creeps some times" I continued.

"Animals is funny sometimes" was all grandpa mumbled.

Archie Matthews

"And grandpa, I never once ever heard them bark, how come they don't ever bark?"

At this last question grandpa's face turned a bit red and he stopped fooling with his contrivance and leaning over the side of his chair he spit tobacco into his spittoon. Then he slowly turned around and looked at me with a funny little twinkle in his eyes all the while, giving grandma a sly sideways glance.

"You noticed that did you? Well, them German's taught their dogs to be real quiet so's they could sneak up on their enemies....Oh, not all of their dogs, but just the extra special spy dogs." He said, real serious like, all the while quickly darting his eyes back and forth to see what grandma's reaction was. But grandma was wresting with the now tangled loops of yarn Trish had set in her chair. She was much to busy with the mess and she had set her ball of yarn down to address the snarl.

Taking what my "all knowing grandfather" had just told me as part of the gospel, I nodded for the reasoning of it and climbed up atop the banister where I usually perched and began to fiddle with my own mechanical contrivance, my cap gun. Pretty soon Trish came back and grandma announced we'd better go get our PJ's on. Even though it wasn't bedtime for another hour, grandma liked kids geared up and ready to go when the time came.

Now, I hated PJ's, and grandma knew it. It was summer and hot anyways, and usually I just went up to bed and stripped down to my birthday suit and slept the way I figured God meant Adam to sleep, before all that Eve and the Snake dealings got us all pitched out of Eden. As far as I was concerned it was too hot to be swathed up in fig leaves, let alone sweltering hot pajamas, but I knew there was no arguing about it, so off I went to my bedroom up stairs to change.

Once again, I was sent off alone to get my changing done and upon my return, Trish then went up and changed, since the only two guest bedrooms were upstairs. I had always slept in the first bedroom atop the stairs and Trish would sleep through the door at the far end of the big bedroom that opened into the smaller bedroom beyond. Since you had to go through the first bedroom to gain access to the second, as you can imagine, it made things a bit awkward when my girl cousin intruded into and through my man cave. Therefore I was doomed to wear PJ's for the next couple of weeks of her visitation, like it or not, hot weather and be danged.

I ran up and changed and upon coming back down, Trish once again exited the front porch and went to do whatever it is young ladies do to change their clothes. It always amazed me that I could change in about two minutes flat, while I'd never known a girl to take less than ten times that amount of time.

The biggest puzzlement was girls wear dresses, and the way I figured it, a dress just came off, "A swoop over the head" and they was done, while a guy, had a separate shirt and pants to deal with. The slow up there being, the shirt had to go up and over, while the pants had to go down and off each leg, even if a guy took his shoes off first, it wasn't as fast a process as I imagined a dress should be.

It wasn't until much later in life that I began to suspect there might be "under things" hampering a female's changing speed. And it wasn't until many years after that and after I'd said, "I do", that I realized just what a process women went through just entering a bathroom, let alone changing. Only then did I have the dawning realization that women actually used all those hair brushes, combs, scent bottles, lotions, shampoos, conditioners, nail trimmers, eye brow pluckers, eyelash curlers…etc., etc. That was about the same time I realized most of what I had been lured into marriage with, was "smoke and mirrors". But of course, by then, as most fisherman realize, after the fish has taken the bait and is quickly pulled up the bank and thumped on the head, it's too late for it to realize what had caught it was just an artificial lure.

Archie Matthews

And after what seemed like an eternity, for grandma had made me her "yarn captive" and I had to take Trish's place holding the loops of yarn on my already exhausted out stretched arms, did Trish finally return. I'd like to say at my age I didn't notice my female cousin's transformation, but I had. Her reddish hair was down instead of pulled and tied back, and it was now sparkling and bushy as a fox's tail and looked nice. I also noticed the full length flannel night gown with little flowers on it. Since I had only brothers and had never seen a girls bed clothes before, I have to say it was more than a little embarrassing, but pretty. Of course it's okay to admit now but back then, I'd have boxed anyone's ears even suggesting I'd notice a girl's appearance, pretty or otherwise.

And seeing my exhausted arm's savior, I quickly got up and held my arms complete with yarn loops out and Trish looped her hands in and relieved me of my burden. Then she sat down and smiled as I slowly backed away still somewhat awed at seeing my older female cousin for what she really was, a pretty young lady.

And then all hell broke loose! No, it wasn't her daddy shooting at me with a shotgun. That didn't take place in my life until in my teenage years and it wasn't my uncle shooting at me. But the results were pretty much the same, there was a whole lot of scrambling and blood curdling screams.

As Trish had sat down, the bottom of her nightgown had slipped up the least bit and revealed her furry slippers, at which time; the pup's also noticed and with their skulks had slipped up the steps and onto the porch unnoticed. Then with a mad rush, each pup grabbed a slipper and that's when our peaceful evening turned to chaos.

Trish's bloodcurdling screams sent grandma into fits of chaos, as the pups sharp little teeth clamped down on each slipper, snarling and savagely shaking her feet as she kicked in panic. I'm not sure if it was the startled mad dash of the dogs, the blood curdling high pitched scream of a redheaded girl, or the wailing

The Pets in the Post

of a frightened old lady, but poor old grandpa swallowed his tobacco and as swallowed tobacco does, it didn't go down quietly.

Grandpa began hacking and coughing doing his utmost to not choke to death on a lump of chewing tobacco midway down his windpipe, all the while trying to jump up out of his chair. Getting half way up, he was suddenly jerked back down. I will say, the old fellow fought valiantly and went through the process a good three or four times before realizing the mechanical crank on the can opener was caught on his shirt and the arm of the chair as he fought to gain his feet.

Between the ensnared shirt front and the offending crank, poor grandpa just kept being stopped midair, half way between sitting and just before he could get a foothold at standing. Then with a baritone bellow, grandpa cleared his windpipe of his tobacco and down it went, while grabbing both chair arms and heaving, up he came.

Just as grandpa gained his feet the pups having secured good grips upon their furry little prizes, each dashed back off the porch, slippers and all. Poor Trish, being relieved of both her slippers and much of her senses, stopped to take a breath and suddenly realized the dog pack attack was over.

The pups dashed right between grandpa's legs and were gone as quickly as they had appeared; I know that because I saw them from where I had fallen off the banister and into the prickly evergreen bushes below. My feet sticking practically straight up and my head down vantage gave me a startling view of up the steps and beneath Trish's nightgown.

Being fifty years old now, I can reflect back on that evening with a smile and a chuckle, but at the time I had been utterly horrified. The horror of two quick shapes dashing upon the porch from the twilight, and me coming to the sudden conclusion I was about to become demon clutched. Trish's scream had all but sent my

Archie Matthews

soul out of my body and half way to heaven before I realized I had no ticket to enter and turned back.

The additional horror of the situation happened to be the quick and sudden realization that Trish's clothing change evidently hadn't been slowed down by "under things", and that's all I am saying about that.

Of course after grandpa got the women settled down, he did come down the steps and dug me out of the evergreens. After helping me get to my feet, grandpa went inside and returned with his flashlight and began to search the darkening yard for the pups and Trish's slippers.

Meanwhile, grandma calmed the still jittery Trish and after a few calm words, she went inside for a few minutes and rustled around and returned to take her seat.
"Come here" grandma crooned sweetly looking at me and motioning with her tender outstretched hand. And like the little inexperienced "rube" I was, I slid into my loving grandmother's outstretched "Clutches"!

For clutches they were, as she laid hold of me and I instantly recognized the small vile bottle of hair raising Mercurochrome. Oh, how I'd like to say I fought and scratched and kicked, but all I could manage at the time was a couple of futile twists and squirms as I tried to get away from the caustic daubing I knew was about to take place.

At this point in the story, I would like to point out I didn't scream and blubber or howl as grandma plucked little barbed ends of evergreen needles out of my hide and then seared my wounds shut with cauterizing dabs of the bright red liquid fire.

Now I am NOT talking about the soft fuzzy bunny liquid called "Iodine". Trust me, if you've ever had your hide cauterized with Mercurochrome and then fairy kissed by Iodine, you would definitely know the difference.

The Pets in the Post

My dear sweet grandmother being the loving grandparent she was, evidently wanted her grandchildren to live a germ free life. The only problem with that, was the old lady had a bit of "Eighteenth Century Torturer" in her. She thought by engulfing the wound with liquid fire, it was a bit like burning Witches, once seared, the evil was dead and gone.

Therefore when the Mercurochrome, liberally applied, began to smoke, cauterize and sear the very soul, it must be killing germs by the droves, as my howling and wailing attested.

My grandpa was fond of saying, "If those are the screeches of the retreating germs, that's a passel of them howling!

Good old grandpa and his joking. I'd have liked to have given him a dose and seen how he'd howl. But although I'd seen the remaining pink spots of Mercurochrome on him from time to time, I'd never heard him bellow about it. I always suspected the crafty old fellow went into a far off room and stuck a piece of leather wrapped stick in his mouth, as they did on the old westerns, to keep from crying out.
More than once I'd searched the medicine cabinet to see if I could lay eyes on an old teeth marked chunk of lead bullet, but all my searches had ever turned up was a startling vast supply of the offending red bottles of liquid misery.

After what seemed like hours of being repeatedly scalded like a cat with boiling water poured in my wounds, grandpa returned with a sad look.

"Well, I found what's left of those slippers" he mumbled as he held out a double fistful of well chewed tatters.

"Oh, that's a shame honey," grandma said as she patted Trish's hand, having paused from her despicable liquid torture.

Immediately recognizing my brief reprieve for what it was, I quickly escaped to the other side of the porch, still holding my smoldering arm dotted as if a thousand lava mosquitoes had

Archie Matthews

bitten me. The pink mercurochrome welting up and around both arms, but the right arm being the freshest scorched was still the most tender of the two. To this day, I can still see and smell the scorching hide I'd sacrificed way back then out on that porch.

I won't go into detail of the long night filled with nightmares of screaming girls with no underwear. I will say, I dreamt of long fanged wild dog attacks and witches dunking me into red lakes of flaming mercurochrome. But never in my wildest dreams did I have a nightmare even close to what I was about to experience that very next day. Well, not until afterwards, for who could ever imagine such horror until it actually happens to you?

Dawn broke and so did I, for upon bailing out of bed, wearing those darn hot pajamas I'd been fully clothed in all night, I headed for the stairs and quickly snagged my shirt cuff on the stair rail and down I went. If you've ever had your lower end in high gear, trying to hurry to breakfast, and suddenly had your upper end jerked to a stop, you'll know I went flat on my back. The resulting crash did two things, knocked all the wind right out of me and brought my still jittery cousin Trish charging from the attached bedroom, half clothed. When I say half clothed, I mean the bottom half, the half I'd already had a horrified gander at the night before.

Now she bolted from her bedroom with some kind of lacey harness strapped around her chest holding things in place. Now remember, I was still just a young boy and had no desire as of yet to see clothed women, let alone unclothed women. And what with me not even having sisters, I had no idea women had such contraptions, nor wished too.

Trish had no more than came out her door and entered my bedroom, when she must have seen and recognized the expression of horror upon my face, realizing she was short a top, she came to a screeching halt and immediately shifted into reverse. I don't know if it was the loud banging of my back coming down on the ceiling above grandma's head, or the loud

The Pets in the Post

sound of Trish's screeching halt, but the door at the bottom of the stairs opened and up came grandma.

"OH MY?!" she shouted as she saw me stretched full length lying flat on my back on the hard stairs, one arm still tangled in my ripped off pajama sleeve as it hung from the banister rail over my head.

Having seen more of Trish than I had ever imagined, or ever wanted too, my eyes were still screwed tightly shut. But now having heard grandma rush to my aid, I suddenly threw them wide open and watched grandma jump about a foot straight up in the air.

"HEAVENS!" she screamed, "What are you doing lying their looking like a dead man and then scaring the daylights out of me with that wild look? Are you some kind of crazy man?!"

After helping me get untangled from the sleeve, grandma told me to get changed and then come to breakfast, "And bring your shirt down so I can mend it." She added as back down the steps she went. That's why I was standing stark naked at the foot of the bed with my pajama bottoms around my ankles and my top laying on the foot of the bed, stretching out to grab my trousers, when Trish got an eyeball full of payback.

When your fifty you can smile and nod with the realization that life has all kinds of twists and turns and fate can be quite fickle. If this terrorizing exchange had taken place just a few years later in my teens, I would have been elated, for I spent many of my teen years searching out the ever elusive half naked female. But as I've said previously, "tit for tat" just wasn't anything I was interested in at all, and Trish's eyeball of payback at the time, still felt like somehow I had gotten the short end of the stick, even with the shocking look of horror upon her face.

Needless to say, after that summer, I and cousin Trish had a very…um…let's say, "Tenuous Friendship". To this day, I'm sure she thought I was some kind of flashing pervert and being the

Archie Matthews

good girl she was, tried her best to be cordial, yet wary as a cat fresh out of scalded water. It was only after our little "Outhouse episode" that I was branded by Trish and her parents as an "Incorrigible juvenile delinquent pervert", but that's another story.

After a very red faced breakfast, with very little chatter from either the "flasher or the flashy", take your pick as to which of us was what at which time, but I can assure you we were both embarrassed. I went outside and Trish stayed inside to help grandma.

I wandered around the house and saw the pups laying in the far corner under the trumpet vine still chewing on some bits of Trish's fuzzy slippers.
That's when I noticed their light brown fur was beginning to get light streaks in it and a silvery look to the tips. But even though I was in grade school and getting fairly good grades, I still couldn't add two plus two and come up with the answer as to why those pups acted and now began to look so strange.

And with a shake of my head and my bladder humming a fast march, I quickly made my way to the outhouse and the morning "Watering of my mules". As I went by the strawberry patch beside the far end of the woodshed on my way out the gate, I noticed the big red breasted Robin fly up with a huge worm in her mouth, perch on the fence, and warily watching me pass. I was quickly reminded of the little birds and decided to come back later at the first opportunity and take a gander at how much they'd grown.

After several minutes of not only "Water 'n mules, but pitch 'n them a bale or two of hay", I finished up the paperwork, fastened up and lurched out the door. And there just out of the gate and coming down the trail, was Trish, coming to give the water closet a visit. Not wanting to have to exchange pleasantries, let alone look her in the eye, I turned a hard right and headed into grandpa's scrap yard between the outhouse and blacksmith shop.

Trish, seeing me shoot out of the outhouse and down the side trail towards the blacksmith shop hesitated for a few instants before proceeding onward. I gave her a quick look over my shoulder and disappeared into the scrap yard.

I tinkered around as kids are wont to do, first riding the old caterpillar and imagining I was moving mountains of earth with the bulldozer, to wandering into one wrecked vehicle and out of another. Soon, I found myself beside the back wall to the shop and that's when I heard two voices talking inside..

Now that blacksmith shop had a back door that wasn't but a few steps down the wall, but that's not what I sidled up to. I had long since discovered a perfectly convenient knothole that happened to be just right for a kid my size to get down on all fours and look or listen into. The inside of the knothole happened to be located between the top of and the middle shelf of grandpa's work bench. Thus allowing a kid to look into and not be seen by an adult standing or even sitting close, for the shop was dark and shadowy, especially beneath that work bench.

As I got down on all fours, I peered in the knothole and saw Eddy Mehan the neighbor across the way that lived in, owned and operated the café. Eddy was just saying, "Well Arch, I don't know how much longer you're going to be able to keep them. They're going to become more and more of a problem the longer they're with you. The young ones are especially curious and troublesome."

"I know Eddy," grandpa began, "But I surely love em both, even if they are troublesome scamps and I know it's just going to get worse."

I was so shocked and hurt, I couldn't even wait to hear anymore and jumped to my feet and ran back up the trail towards the outhouse. I came up the trail about the same time I saw Trish come out of the "Water Closet" looking me over with a wary sidelong glance.

Archie Matthews

"Trish, wait up…" I half shouted then realized I didn't want grandpa to hear me or see me with Trish.

"Trish, we need to talk…..we got serious trouble." I blurted out coming to a halt just a few feet away.

Trish's face began to turn a bit red and she said, "What do you think we need to talk about?"

"I just heard grandpa say we were troublesome scamps and he knows we're going to get worse, and maybe they should get rid of us." I groaned, more than a bit worried.

"Well….." Trish whispered as she began wringing her hands together "we are getting older and I seen my older brother Danny go through the 'Peek' n and stalk 'n stage' as pa put it. I got brothers and I've seen all I ever needed to see, but you're a boy and pa says boys just get into that stage and go nuts. So I don't know why they'd want to get rid of me. If their feeling the need to rid themselves of a troublesome scamp, I reckon they're going to get rid of you. Besides, I'm just here until ma and pa come home; you're here till the end of summer break."

Talk about cut from the herd and abandoned, I felt lower than low, cut to the bone and then mad under the collar and I spoke right up.

"And it wasn't even my fault!" I wailed, "You're the one that come barreling out while I was told to get changed! How come it's always the guy that's blamed?" and up the trail to the house I stormed, leaving my cousin the female Benedict Arnold alone with her sins upon the outhouse trail. Little did I know my prophesy of "always the guy getting blamed" would be the story of my life growing up.

I needed a place to think and knew it wouldn't be in the house with grandma and Trish, and I had no hankering to go down to the blacksmith shop where Eddy and grandpa plotted cutting my summer vacation short. I hesitated for a minute and actually

The Pets in the Post

thought about going inside the woodshed. Yet, although this was a life crisis, it didn't warrant sacrificing myself to a bloody demise at the hand of the monster's within. And so with that idea quickly scrapped, I saw the pups eyeballing me from beneath the trumpet vine and I quickly decided to join them.

I went to the corner of the yard and crawled up under the hanging trumpet vine and was immediately astonished at seeing a long pathway along the fence secretly hidden from anyone in the yard. My jaw dropped at realizing what an amazing hiding spot this was. The trail ran along the whole fence beneath the far reaching trumpet vine. I slowly crawled on my hands and knees and began down the path, the two pups staying just out of arms reach ahead. After covering several yards, suddenly the pups stopped and their heads went up as did their ears and crawling closer, I saw a large fat bull snake coiled in the trail.

Since I'd caught many a water snake as well as bull snakes and knew without a doubt the difference between venomous and non-venomous snakes, I knew it was only the pup's instincts that kept them at bay. I quickly found a stick and poked the fat bull snake out of the way, keeping a watchful eye as it slithered off.

Although non-venomous, bull snakes still had teeth and would bite if provoked, I knew better than to try and pick up a bull snake. Water snakes on the other hand, had itsy bitsy teeth that they rarely bit with, let alone broke the skin, while a bull snake's best defense was to coil up and act like a rattle snake. I'd even seen bull snakes shake their tails as if to mimic rattlers, I'd also seen them strike at dogs and cats and more than once I'd caught them by pinning them with a stick and putting them in a large gallon jar.

Having run off the bull snake, the pups and I went on down the trail and soon came to an old rug that evidently the pups had acquired and drug under here for a bed. They both plopped down as if right at home and watched me crawl on down the trail. The trail was a long ways on hands and knees, and I was astounded at how spacious it was beneath that broad canopy of

Archie Matthews

the huge trumpet vine. The trumpet vine looked big from the yard, for it completely covered the full length of the fence, including up and over the trellis above the gate, which was the only real break in the trail beneath.

The fence was a good five foot high and made of wooden slats. The vine along the road side was not dangling clear down to the ground as it was on the inside, there was no trail on the street side. But the wooden slat fence was set close together and shielded prying eyes from that side, making the trail beneath the trumpet vine a kid's hidden paradise.

I don't know how long I was exploring under the vine, before it came to me that this was the perfect hiding place for plunder. I began to sneak back and forth from the vine to the house slowly moving a pocket of toys into my new hiding spot as well as the rug off the back porch and a few odds and ends here and there. Once I had everything under the vine, I began to set up house. It wasn't long before I had a cozy little spot just like the pups had. I had my own rug to sit cross legged Indian style on, as well as my cap gun, which I could poke ever so slightly through the leaves at passersby and pretend I "Bumped them off" from ambush.

Before I knew it, I was soon being hailed by Trish and called for lunch. I was just around the corner and knew I couldn't be seen; therefore I jumped to my feet and ran to the house. After eating lunch with grandma, grandpa and Trish, I once again went back outside and decided to explore my new hideaway back towards the woodshed.

I quickly ducked beneath the trumpet vine and began crawling up the other side from the gate towards the far corner and around it to the woodshed. As I rounded the corner, I found a small hole in this section of the back fence, which happened to be wire. The large square wire holes allowed a lot more view through the fence to the other side than the wooden slats did and therefore also being no road along that side, there was another large hidden expanse along that side of the fence. Using a pair of pliers I'd secretly "Borrowed" from granddads shop when he

The Pets in the Post

wasn't looking, I enlarged the hole to where it was big enough for me to crawl through. This hole allowed me to enter the back pasture and slip around the corner of the woodshed to its backside. There a fellow could access the outhouse and the scrap yard with ease through the waist high grass and weeds of the pasture, unseen by anyone in the house or yard.

I had spent most of the day in jubilant surprise at finding such a magnificent spy tunnel that gave me visible access to anyone in the side, back and front yard without ever being seen. It also gave me a tunnel way I could crawl from the front yard down the side yard and to the woodshed, allowing me to escape out back without ever being spotted. To a kid this was better than James Bond gadgets, this was real life right here in my yard, well at least, my grandparents yard.

And then as I stepped back around the other corner of the woodshed, I could look over the fence and into the strawberry garden and rounding the corner of the yard, I could step into the outhouse trail and off to the outhouse to my right, or turn left and go back into the yard through the gate.

I was standing at the gate grinning from ear to ear at my spectacular discovery totally unaware my magnificent afternoon was about to take a dramatic turn for the worse. The first thing that I noticed out of place, were the pups sniffing along the yard side by side right up and stopping at the clothes line post. This gave me a pause for thought, for I'd never seen them sniff along in such a defined straight line before. Then I notice the Robin screeching and having a fit from a nearby tree limb. She was acting very strange as she would hop from branch to branch and screech and squawk like she always did when I went to pet her babies, except, I wasn't.

The pups had stopped and were looking up the clothes line post and the old mother Robin was hopping around scolding when I came up with the bright idea of visiting my little "Pets in the post". So without much fanfare, other than that from the old squawking

Archie Matthews

mother Robin, I quickly fetched out the old wobbly chair and climbed up it and reached into the top of the post.

Right up until this exact second, life was good, the day was sweet smelling, the sun shone bright and the world was spinning up right and at the proper speed. But the instant I stuck my hand over that edge, everything changed. Suddenly I smelled a strange odor and as I felt the movement inside the nest, I felt a lump, but somehow it was very different, for it was smooth and I didn't feel the feathers I should have.

A split second decision was made and I was half a milli-second from withdrawing my empty hand from the strange slick moving thing my fingers briefly felt, when my foot slipped from the wooden side of the chair to the rotting cane seat in the middle.

At that moment, if God had frozen time, and asked me which fate I would like to suffer, and explained which avenue each trail of fate ended with, I'd have taken the "Fall flat on my face" option. But God didn't see fit to stop time and ask me those questions, nor give me my choice of options. What he had seen fit to do, was give me choice making reflexes that decided for me.

And as my foot proceeded through the rotten cane seat, my retreating hand took on an adventurous mind of its own and instead of coming back empty, had closed and came back full of smooth hide and wriggling terror. This was also about the time that the world stopped spinning up right and changed to a slower speed, for suddenly up became down as I headed over backwards in slow motion towards the ground.

The slow motion allowing my "Still at normal speed eyeballs" to swivel up and take in what was now wrapping its engorged long belly and tail around my grasping hand and forearm. For as you might have guessed , I held in my grasp, the even fatter bull snake, that was even now wrapping it's self around my arm.

The Pets in the Post

As I hit the ground and the air was immediately knocked out of my scream mechanism, I could only lay for a second fighting for breath and work my silent mouth in quiet horror.

With my mouth wide open, and my scream mechanism waiting for air to push through at high volume, my eyes once again shot to my still clutched fingers. I immediately began sending signals from my brain to my fingers to abandon ship and get the hell out of there! But along with the signal to my lungs from my brain desperately relaying the empty working scream mechanisms request for air, the signals seemed to be taking "FOREVER"!

And then to heap injury upon insult Mr. Bull Snake evidently feeling so rudely interrupted at his dinner table, decided two robin chicks weren't enough, but he also needed some desert and decided my hand might fit the bill. I very distinctly remember that mouth of his gaping wide and his evil black eyes twinkling as he sank his fangs in my hand at the exact second both signals were received and answered by hand and lungs alike.

I don't know which split second happened first, the air hitting my scream mechanism with a vengeance, or my fingers instantly deciding they needed to be somewhere other than wrapped around an un-happy and protesting bull snake. Whichever came first, I can attest without hesitation the next thing that happened was my left hand came to the immediate defense of the right. My left hand shot over and grabbed the whipping bull snake by the tail and quickly getting to my feet, and shaking my leg to dislodge the still clinging chair, I took up my deadly fighting stance and the battle began in earnest.

Normally a slithering, whipping, slick skinned bull snake might be hard to get a grasp on, put this instance was nothing even remotely "Normal". For this evil snake had two large lumps like the handy knots put in a rope allowing a climber a good grip. And it was the closest lump to the tail that I grasped and pulled with all my terror filled might.

Archie Matthews

That Bull Snake evidently decided it did not like being mistaken for a huge elastic band and stretched to the far reaches of the galaxy, for he quickly spat out my hand and came unwrapped with my mighty pull.

What fickle fate had so precisely timed that very instance for my precious cousin Trish to come to the back door to see what all the screaming was about, I'll never know. I've often smiled ruefully to think it was a bit of payback for her interrupting my serene summer break with her very presence…let alone the "up the dress and the gawking" she'd subjected me to.

Whatever the case may be, as she came to the back porch and opened the screen, I cracked that un-wound bull snake like a mule skinner cracks a bull whip and out shot that devoured half-digested little bird.

If it had been a thrown rock, or a stone from a sling shot, or even a rifle or pistol shot, anyone would have shouted "Bulls eye", at any other time or target, but it was not to be this time or with cousin Trish as the unspecified, not to mention unwilling target. I will say, if it had been a rifle or pistol shot, it couldn't have achieved more startling effects, for as that little bird splattered against Trish's forehead with a "Splat", she toppled over as if struck dead, head over heels backwards.

Grandma having been right behind her stopped in her tracks at seeing her niece fall over backwards apparently stone dead with what appeared like brain matter stuck to her forehead. She screamed the most ear piercing scream I've ever heard before or since and pray I will never hear the likes of again. And had it been any other female, I am sure they too would have immediately joined Cousin Trish prone upon the porch, but my grandma was molded from much sterner stuff. She stayed upright for one more crack of the bull snake and was only saved being caught in the lower abdomen by the second and somewhat smaller and squishier ejected tweedy, by the returning screen door. For Trish had pushed that screen door open enough that its returning spring only now slammed it shut just in

The Pets in the Post

time to shield grandma from the worst of the splattering projectiles that smacked into and somewhat through the course mesh screen.

Although grandma's stout constitution had kept her upright even though her beloved niece had just fallen dead before her very eyes, seeing the half devoured remains of a whipping snake disgorged before her very eyes must have weakened the old girls knees, for they buckled.

Well, buckled probably isn't a very good description, for actually after the horrified look on her face and having her eyes roll to the back of her head, she more like careened over, than buckled. Needless to say, she went down and went down with a bang.

Having made two hard cracks with the bull snake with remarkable results, at which time the snake was still wiggling, I quickly gave him the "Coup'de'gra" and smacked him around that clothesline post a couple times. And with every complete wrap around the clothesline post and the resulting sound of a wet rope getting it's just do, I felt his evil bite had been avenged.

Dropping my "limp as a noodle" attacker, I quickly approached the back porch to see what all the bodies piling up was all about. At that same time grandpa came thundering through the front door across the living room and stood with his own look of astonishment from me to the bodies of grandma and Trish.

As if my poor nerves hadn't been through enough, suddenly Trish's eyes flashed open and with a scream she sat up right and jumped to her feet. All I can say, is I sure was glad to still be on the other side of the closed screen door. She gave me a look as I imagine many a murdered victim has witnessed from their maniacal killer, just seconds before their demise. Then with a growl and out stretched claws, she leapt towards the door that separated us.

Now I haven't lived to the ripe old age of fifty that I am today by being a slow poke, and I'd learned to move with lightning

Archie Matthews

lifesaving speed early in my childhood, and it was this kind of swift lifesaving action that saved me at that précised moment. For instantly recognizing death when I saw it, especially this close and merely separated by a screen door, I also leapt forward and put my foot and both hands to the screen door and pushed to keep it closed with every fiber of my being. To this day, I am amazed that flimsy wooden screen door held back the maniac that seemed bent on my destruction long enough for grandpa to come to his senses and save me.

Grandpa was about to have his own hands full I noticed as grandma's eyes blinked and battered open and she sat up and joined in with Trish's irate jargon as both women began to prophesize my demise and subsequent fiery destination once I fell into their clutching, grasping claws.

I have to give it to grandpa the man could calm a crowd, even this female lynch mob. Once he got everyone to realize nobody was seriously hurt, other than mentally traumatized, which trust me, in my family is nothing out of the ordinary, he got everyone to sit down in the dining room. Although I was by far the most reluctant to enter the cramped quarters with the two still growling, ferocious looking females, their fingers ever curling and un-curling, just itching to get around my throat.

But, with grandpa's assurance that "nobody was going to be allowed to butcher anyone… now or in the near future", I slowly edged inside and sat down. I do have to admit, I kept my main spring wound up tight with my finger on the trigger ready to fire myself into and through the very wall if necessary to gain the outside. I imagined grandma as "Death" and Trish as "Destruction". After all grandma was older and wiser and had more experience I imagined killing things quick, while Trish was young and being less experienced might waste all kinds of time beating me and pulverizing my bones while I lingered on.

To conclude this little chapter of the "Pet's in the Post", I won't bore you with the hour long recited explanation to grandpa of why I had been standing in the back yard whipping half-digested dead birds out of a bull snake at Trish and Grandma. There may or may not have been some added explanatory embellishment trying to soften the blows to my backside that I knew without a doubt would be coming.

I also won't go into detail about how I was grounded and under close scrutiny of everyone within a quarter mile of our house, for word got around quick in that little town. I couldn't go to "Water my mules" without a dozen pair of eyes on me there and back again.

Do you have any idea how hard it is to water mules when you know you're being watched? It's not easy, let me tell you. Let alone pitch them a bale or two when the need arises.

I can say, when Uncle Tick and Aunt Edna returned for their darling daughter, you could tell Trish had missed them terrible, for she cried and cried and clung to them as if she was scared to death they were going to go and leave here there even for the briefest of moments. It was only the next summer that I fully felt the fallout from Trish's tattling to anyone and everyone in and out of the family about our little mishaps.

As for grandma and grandpa, they loved me and were the best of grandparents, although I have to say, when my parents came to get me later that summer, they seemed a bit relieved if not glad, to have me go home. Although I was often warned by grandma she was going to tell my dad what I'd done, she never did. And despite the stripped almost bare, willow tree down behind the outhouse, I still loved grandma despite my being somewhat "un-fond" of her right arm and its willow switching abilities. She was a kind little old lady with a heart of gold, but she could wield a willow switch that would startle a butcher as she'd cut meat off the bone quicker than any band saw or meat cleaver.

And grandpa, he was more than a bit sad about all the "molested little critters". He buried what was left of both the half eaten little tweedy birds, with the mother Robin looking on. He also dug a

Archie Matthews

hole and gently coiled up the remains of the bull snake, whipped to a frazzle though he was.

Oh, and the pups……did you guess? Yup, they turned out to be young Coyotes. The sneaking little wild scamps. Trish's slippers might have been their first attack, but it surely wasn't their last, by any means. And grandpa kept the secret from grandma until one evening she'd awoke with howling coyotes barking at their very bedroom window, and it was either tell her the truth or go out with a gun and fend off the prowling pack, and we all know grandpa wouldn't do that.

So he'd spilled the beans about old Tucker Sexton up on Third Fork crick seeing the old mother coyote at the opening to her den and shooting her before he knew she had the pups. Tucker being a woodsman and having respect for wildlife as most, had brought the pups to grandpa and been sworn to secrecy.

The pups stayed with the grand folk's for a couple more summers before grandpa decided he'd either better take them back to the far reaches or risk the even farther reaches of the law. For several neighbors began to complain about coyotes getting into their chicken houses at night, meanwhile grandma's flower beds began to sprout chicken feathers.

And the Clothesline post? Yup, almost every single year a red breasted Robin would have a nest of chicks there. And "Yup" every year I'd take a look…..from a well-placed ladder supplied by grandpa…..it was part of our settlement agreement with grandma. But I had to promise grandpa to only look and keep my hands to myself. After all, it was an easy promise to both make and keep, for I'd touched all I wanted for many years to come. Well, that is, until I was a teenager and drove up to the lake that one night with a girlfriend, but that's another story.

And now that we've come all the way around that severely beaten bush, we've come to the END of my story. Thanks for listening….or should I say reading?

The Stink Eye

Festus was the name of Marshall Dillon's deputy on the old western television series called Gun Smoke, but it was also the name given to my grandmother's small white terrier. Festus was the epitome of Gun Smoke's deputy; he had the scruffy whiskers, the squinty eye and sauntered around like he was the duly elected law and order of both yard and home.

Nary a human nor critter approached the fence around the property, let alone entered the premises, but what Festus didn't show up to check it out, his bark and bite as ready for the fast draw as ever a western deputies side arm. As long as the visitor was friendly, old Festus would live and let live, but let that visitor start trouble, and Festus always gave as good as he got. Well, that is until one faithful evening when poor old Festus bit off more than he could chew, or so the saying goes.

Grandma and grandpa loved that little dog. Festus was a small wire haired terrier that they had gotten from old man Wellner's herd of dogs. Yes, that's what I said; the man had a "herd" of dogs. I never saw him but what he didn't have a herd of at least fifteen to twenty dogs with him. Usually they filled the back of his old blue truck that smoked as if it's under carriage was on fire.

My grandparents lived in the little town of Ola, Idaho and my granddad ran the local Blacksmith shop. The Wellner's lived up the lane in the little valley that ran up behind town. Everyone adored and spoke very highly of Mrs. Wellner, but when it came to her husband George, everyone just smiled and circled their index finger around their temple and gave a knowing wink. George was a might "touched", or so my grandmother had explained the hand motion to me one time.

Nobody ever actually said he was "crazy", for people respected the Wellners and always remarked about what fine folks they were. It's just George was "cut from a different kind of cloth" as my granddad put it. As a kid, If I'd ever had to describe what kind of cloth he might have been cut from, I'd have to say it was one of them wild colored tie dyed cloths…..the man had color, strange though he was, he was never plain or drab.

But my granddad had explained to me once that George, as he called him by his first name, but to me he was Mr. Wellner, had once been just like everyone else and held all his cards upstairs; But there had been some kind of "Unfortunate hunting accident" that had left the man a card or two short of a full deck. Mr. Wellner's mental state never bothered me, for although he was a might different than most adults, they all seemed crazy as loons to me, but Mr. Wellner was always good to me and every other kid I ever knew.

George came to town one day in his old blue pickup full of dogs. You could hear that pickup a mile away coming down the little valley road headed into town. That old blue pickup smoked like a house fire and rattled so loud it reminded me of a herd of cooks with their aprons on fire, beating and banging their pans in hopes of being doused. If that hadn't been noise enough, that truckload of dogs bayed and bellowed like their tails where caught in a screen door. They'd start bellowing the moment they saddled up and they never shut up until the old man parked that truck. I'd always come a running to see the show, as did

The Stink Eye

everyone else in town, for when old George drove his truck to town, it was a spectacle.

Hearing that truck coming down the valley, I shouted at grandma "Mr. Wellner's a come 'n!" and I ran outside to the gate to watch the show.

Sure enough, here come the huge black blue cloud of smoke down the road with just the hint of headlights and a metal grill poking out front. The sound of the dogs and the rattling old truck just about deafened me as it roared by the yard.

As always, I was amazed dogs didn't fly out everywhere as it turned the corner so fast it went up on two wheels. Flying around the corner and sailing past the house and then by granddad's blacksmith shop, that pickup was in town and out of town in the blink of an eye. And as always, Mr. Wellner never paid a lick of attention to the one single stop sign we had in the town, as he sailed right through it on his way up the hill on the far side of town.

Of course the town of Ola at that time barely consisted of a quarter mile stretch of road that connected at both ends to the main road, with but the one stop sign at the upper end. At the lower far end there was a little white church and a cemetery, then the stock yards of Ace' and then his and Marge's house, while across the street was Ed Shotz' general store with two gas pumps in front.

Then there was my grandparent's home across the little side street that Mr. Wellner had just come down. Then next to that was granddads Blacksmith shop and across the road from that were Eddy Mehan and his wife Elaine's Café/gas station, also with two fuel pumps outside. It was the only little town I'd ever seen that didn't even have a bar or Tavern, although Eddy did serve a cold beer in the café'.

A crowd had gathered on the front porch of the general store and another small group of people had collected at the Café'/gas

Archie Matthews

station as the truck sped by in a cloud of smoke and dogs in full bark mode.

As the truck began to climb the small hill just north of town, the engine cut out and the truck began to slow down. The only way anyone could tell the motor had stopped was the sudden ceasing of the billowing smoke, for the rattle of the truck parts continued as did the loud barking of a truckload of dogs.

The old truck coasted almost to the top of the hill and then slowly came to a stop and sat for the briefest of moments, before it began rolling backwards down to the gas station. Seeing the truck coming back down the hill backwards and headed right towards the gas pumps, sent a panicked ripple through the group gathered there. I wouldn't say they actually fled for their lives, but I would say, they vacated the vicinity of the gas pumps rapidly. Some ran inside the station and others ran across the street to the front of the blacksmith shop. But as usual, every eye was peeled and glued upon the fast approaching truck.

As the truck coasted backwards to the station it had slowed down considerably, and just before it actually reached the fuel pumps, it swerved the slightest bit and edged to the side, instead of backing over them. Upon coming even with the pumps, out jumped a gray-haired old man and running to the back of the pickup, he threw down the tailgate, grabbed a huge rock and thrust it behind the rear tire, bringing the vehicle to a stop. Then with another quick move, he produced another large rock from amongst the herd of dogs in the back, and wedged it before a front tire.

"I guess that's a poor man's emergency brake," I heard one of the spectators from the store shout amidst a bunch of laughter.

Mr. Wellner stood up with a beaming smile just as the dogs stopped barking as all motion of the truck ceased. I don't know if it was to celebrate Mr. Wellner's coming to town, the successful stop with his elaborate breaking system before wiping out the gas pumps and exterminating the town, or the dogs ceasing their bellowing, but everyone suddenly cheered. Even grandpa standing in front of his blacksmith shop with his big friendly smile, for he and Mr. Wellner were good friends and he always cheered his arrival as well.

My grandmother was at the other end of the spectrum and not much of a fan of Mr. Wellner, although she and Mrs. Wellner were good friends. Often, I'd heard grandma remark, "That George! I don't know how such a good family came by such a bad nut?"

Today it seemed she held fast to that opinion, for there she stood on the front porch, shaking her head wringing her hands in her apron, grandma looked down at me standing inside the gate and read my mind. "Yes, you can go down to the shop, just mind those dogs and don't get bit."

I quickly exited through the front gate and charged over to Mr. Wellner and his herd of dogs. Those dogs were the friendliest bunch of mixed breeds ever known to man. My grandmother always predicted they were one day going to devour a kid or begin killing livestock, but the only thing I'd ever seen those dogs kill was time in the shade on a hot day, furthermore, the only thing they ever threatened to devour was when they nearly licked a kid to death or someone dropped food.

I'd dropped a half-eaten hot dog once, while crossing the street from the café' back to the blacksmith shop, and there had instantly been such a dog pile, as you only hear about in fairy tales. One minute I was walking across the empty dirt road, and the next moment I was surrounded by dogs clear up to my eyeballs. Although sudden and a bit of a shock, there hadn't been anything scary about it, they were a friendly bunch, that is, unless you were the hot dog.

Mr. Wellner always claimed "Their as fine a pack'o hunt 'n dogs as ever graced the planet".

Archie Matthews

And I'd heard it told over to the store around the potbellied stove last winter, "Old George and his dog's had treed a big old sow bear" and then the laughter had broken out and someone had shouted, "Yup, and outcome the ba'r, and darn near eat George, dogs and all!" the laughter hadn't diminished until my grandmother had hustled me out of there and we were back across the street.

"Lay'abouts!" she had hissed, for that's what she always called the group men that collected in the back of the store, and as you can imagine, grandma had a dim view of lay'abouts.

I skidded up to the back of the truck and instantly became the victim of an avalanche of licking and frolicking like the world has never seen, as that mountain of dogs poured out of the truck on top of me.

There were at least two huge Russian wolf hounds, a couple of collies, a Sheppard or two, and both a black and golden lab. There were three beagles, a Bassett hound and two or three Weiner dogs. It's always hard to sort out just how many Weiner dogs were in that herd, due to their long bodies, it's so hard to tell where they stop and another dog begins.

I also noticed several dogs of various breeds that I didn't recognize and therefore just labeled them "Mutt's". Every one of them juggled and jostled for a pat and an ear scratch from me, before following Mr. Wellner over to the blacksmith shop.

My granddad shook Mr. Wellner's hand and they exchanged pleasantries and then retreated into the cool shadows of the shop. The dogs on the other hand, instinctively stopped at the door as if it were an electrified barrier. Then as if by command, they spread out all along the shaded front of the shop, like an army troop on brief furlough awaiting further orders.

As the crowds began to disperse, I wandered over and in the blacksmith shop to listen to grandpa and Mr. Wellner catch up on old times. Grandpa quickly banked the coal fire in his blacksmith

The Stink Eye

forge and settled down for some visiting. Pulling up an old wooden chair for Mr. Wellner, he then sat on the rough wooden nail keg he kept beside his work bench.

I won't bore you with all the stories that those two old timers swapped. I can assure you they covered quite a broad spectrum of topics, from livestock to automobiles, to pastries the wives had cooked, to critters they'd shot or run over recently and everything in between. I sat off to the side and listened intently for anything a kid my age might use. A boy never knew what kind of tidbit he might hear and take advantage of.

Like when Mr. Kenny had told grandpa a month ago about his peach trees ripening down by the crick. Now that was information a kid my size could sink his teeth into, and I did, repeatedly until I'd eaten so many peaches I couldn't even consider breaking wind, without running to the outhouse, just in case.

Grandpa and Mr. Wellner's talk ambled around a bit before it landed on something interesting and I instantly perked up and tuned in. It seemed Mrs. Wellner had "Laid down the Law" and insisted that Mr. Wellner, "Get rid of some of those dogs!" When Mr. Wellner told grandpa about how he was going to have to get rid of a dog or two, you'd have thought he'd been ordered to throw his first born child under a moving bus. He sat there with his head down, his eyes sad, wringing his big calloused hands.

"I just don't know what to do with em.....I can't just abandon one of my boys." He moaned. "It just ain't human, a wife up and tell a man to shuck one of his boys. Did you ever hear tell of a more hard hearted thing for a woman to do.....have ya Arch?....Have ya?"

I remember grandpa doing his best to try and console poor Mr. Wellner. I must say, he did a fair job of representing both sides of the argument, and I thought if Mrs. Wellner had been there, she'd have thought so too. But little did I know my limited experience with women, wasn't enough to even come close to

Archie Matthews

what kind of inkling a woman might have in her mind. Let alone a genuine thought, nor would I for about another hundred and eighty five years....or so, I still imagine.

After a while, grandpa realized nothing seemed to help, and leaning over he reached between the brick forge and the back wall of the shop. After fumbling around a few seconds, grandpa pulled out as dusty a wad of burlap as I've ever seen. With a bit of unraveling, there amidst the burlap sprouted an old cork stoppard "Dimmy John". You know the kind, a dark topped clay jug with a single finger hole. Then with a "Swish", and a grunt of satisfaction upon hearing that it still held plenty of liquid, grandpa offered it over to Mr. Wellner.

An instant ago Mr. Wellner had looked like he'd lost his last friend, but upon discovering a new friend in the contents of that whiskey jug, his smile quickly returned and he licked his lips. After a few consolatory sips, Mr. Wellner squinted up one eye and said, "You know Arch, I noticed you ain't got a dog no more."

"Well George, "grandpa explained "Our old dog passed this last winter and we just ain't got another."

Mr. Wellner smiled, "Well now's a good time to pick one out, I got a few for you to choose from and it'd sure help me out. I don't reckon they'd have a finer home than with you folks, and I could come by for a visit once't in a while."

And the next thing I knew we were outside and grandpa was looking over the herd. After walking up and down the line of lounging dogs, his eyes settled on the scruffiest of the lot. There alongside the shop, a laying in the shade, was a small, white, wire haired terrier with a squinty eye and a stubbed tail. If he'd been entered in an ugly dog contest, and I'd have been the judge I'd have picked him too. He was blue ribbon ugly.

Grandpa knelt down and began to reach out and pick him up, but stopped when the feisty rascal jumped to his feet, bared his sharp little yellow teeth and growled, punctuating his contempt with every hair standing straight on end, including his stumpy tail. That little fellow was a scrapper and I reckon he figured grandpa wanted to tangle and he seemed ready to oblige. For although that herd of dogs dearly loved kids, it seemed they weren't all friendly towards adults, especially this ugly tough little customer.

"Here now!" George growled, and reaching down, he picked the little grouch up and handed him to grandpa. The minute Mr. Wellner had spoken; the little mutt had dropped all his "Rabid dog" pretenses and gone back to being a happy go lucky fellow. Grandpa took him and held him out at arm's length and said "He'll do."

Mr. Wellner grunted with satisfaction and his beaming smile let both grandpa and the grouchy little dog know, it was settled. Then with his broad smile and a nod he headed for his truck, his herd of dogs close to his heels. "Take good care of that hunt 'n dog, he's a trained ba'r killer if there ever was one." Mr. Wellner called over his shoulder tickled to have found a good home for one of his "boys".

And with a wave, he quickly loaded up his rocks, jumped in his pickup and was off in a clattering cloud of smoke, complete with dogs in full bark mode, wheeling a U-turn in the middle of Main Street, making me and grandpa jump back for fear of getting run over. Dogs howling and the pickup sounding like it was about to shake apart, and back up and around the hair pin corner he sailed as fast as that billowing cloud of black blue smoke could go.

It seemed the now dispersed crowds didn't notice Mr. Wellner's going as much as they'd noticed his coming, for no one cheered or waved him off, he was just gone in a big puff of smoke and barking dogs; Leaving me and grandpa the only ones watching his disappearing smoke cloud receding up the little ravine road.

After watching him go, I turned towards Grandpa and saw he held out a shiny quarter. "You better go get yourself a soda pop." He said. And I didn't hang around to argue as I took the quarter and headed for the store. Little did I know that was grandpa's way of getting me out of his hair, while he went and did some explaining to grandma about the new addition to the family.

I don't know what he said to her or what transpired, but when I got back to the house with my half drank soda in hand, I saw grandma sitting there in her chair on the front porch just knitting away, the little scruffy rascal curled up right beside her. You'd have thought that dog had known grandma his whole life for he'd settled right in.

Grandpa sat in his chair and just chuckled, "Well, I guess he knows whose dog he is. And that was that, the scruffy little dog and grandma were inseparable from that day on. It wasn't long and grandma started calling him "Festus" after the television show character and everyone smiled at just how well the name fit.

Shortly afterwards me and Festus made friends, since I was the only kid around, and it didn't take him long to realize what a substantial food source a kid is. Old Festus knew real quick which side of his bread was buttered, and although he made it quite clear he was grandma's dog, he wasn't too proud to put up with me and any food I might drop.

Now Festus wasn't much for playing with kids, he seemed to think kids were a necessary evil that had to be tolerated. He wasn't a fetch the stick kind of dog, and only growled every time I even went near a stick, let alone picked one up and shook it at him. He was more of a "watch dog" and by that I mean, he'd just lay around watching until he saw someone coming or heard the gate rattle. The instant someone showed up he was instantly on "Bark Duty" and telling the whole world about it.

Oh and how the little rascal watched. I swear he'd skulk around watching me until he knew I was up to something I didn't want grandma to know about, and then he'd start barking his little tattle. And sure enough, here'd come grandma to see what was

The Stink Eye

up. I don't know how many times the little snitch turned me in. It always seemed just about the time I'd stick my toe in to test the water of an adventure and before I could even begin getting into trouble, the evil little warning bell would go off. It wasn't long, before I began to detest that little tattle tale.

Being a thinking human being and him just a dumb dog, I caught on real quick to keeping a chunk of cookie in my pocket and at the first sign of an impending bark, I'd throw him his extortion morsel and he'd forget all about snitching.

That's how our first summer together went, he'd creep around watching and I'd end up feeding him all my deserts snuck from the table in my pockets. If I'd known where a deep hole had been, and could have gotten him close, I'd have pushed his tattle tale deep inside and been done with him. That summer was a testy one and only years later did I really learn to love the little mutt, but isn't that usually the way it goes.

Festus settled right into spending the summer with us, and we with him.
It was a couple mornings later, right after breakfast when grandma sent me to the woodshed to replenish the wood box in the kitchen, that Festus met "Bob" grandpa's old tom cat.

I opened up the back door and stepped out as Festus shot between my legs on our way to the woodshed. I opened up the woodshed when out popped, Bob.

You'd have thought we'd suddenly been attacked by a full grown cougar, as Festus gave a "Yelp!" wheeled around and ran for his life. All I can say, is it's a good thing Bob hadn't been a full grown cougar, for suddenly it became "every critter for himself" and I would have been an abandoned cougar snack.

Bob, on the other hand, suddenly and quite unexpectantly coming face to face with a strange dog, shot straight up into the air. Luckily, Bob, concluding his sudden moon launch, hit the ground and didn't land atop of me. For with all his claws immediately deployed and ready to shred everything he came into contact with, he too quickly voted for the "every critter for itself" tactic and suddenly vacated the vicinity. And off he went dashing around the side of the woodshed and heading in the opposite direction Festus had just taken.

I still snicker recalling Mr. Wellner's comment about Festus being a "Bear dog". After all, I suppose there is quite a difference between a bear and a house cat. But I could only imagine the kind of hasty retreat Festus would beat if he'd ever met anything bigger than Bob. Little was I to know just such an encounter was right up around the corner and was going to end much different than this one had.

I got a big laugh out of that first meeting, but knew it wouldn't be their last. And that evening on the front porch, I told grandma and grandpa about Bob and Festus's first meeting and we all got a laugh.

Grandma said "I sure hope Festus doesn't run poor old Bob off. He's always been a good mouser and I'd surely hate to lose him."

Grandpa just scoffed, "Don't you worry a bit. Old Bob can hold his own." And grandpa gave me a knowing wink.

All that next day Festus acted strangely on edge. He'd slowly crept around, intently looking into and under ever bush and behind every plant in the yard. He even peered up into the trees, constantly searching for something. Little did I know he was still thinking about that unexpected cougar attack the day before and was on constant watch for another ambush.

That paranoid little mutt spent all afternoon creeping around with his stubby tail straight up in the air, his little legs quivering when he'd creep up to the edge of a bush or the flower bed. He was hilarious as he waded into and through grandma's strawberry patch, the plants no bigger than large coffee cups and unable to hide even a tiny kitten, let alone a full grown cat. But Festus

The Stink Eye

went up and down the rows checking beneath each strawberry, right in front of me, for I was stalking ripe strawberries myself, and not the least bit interested or worried about finding a cougar or a tom cat.

Later that afternoon, I about died laughing when Festus was staring into a cluster of flowers as if it was about to sprout a Bengal tiger, when an unsuspecting bird dropped from the nearby tree to the ground but a foot away. That bird no more than touched down and Festus shot straight up into the air with a startled "yelp" then hit the ground acting like he was some kind of rabid timber wolf. He ran in a circled and barked and growled and tore at the grass with his little clawed feet all stiff legged. If it had been a Bengal tiger attack, we might have actually stood a chance, for all the fight the little bugger put into his display. And then upon looking around and realizing it had just been a bird, and there was no huge dog eating feline around, he gave a "Huff" and wandered off to check out the front yard.

Festus's reaction kind of puzzled me, for I had witnessed his surprise meeting with Bob the tom cat, and seen him tuck what was left of his little stub tail and run like a "fraidy cat". But now the little rascal had evidently bunched up his courage and seemed to be actually looking for a fight. I couldn't help but giggle to think about how that might turn out, if ever he actually caught Bob. I'd seen that old Tom cat tackle a full grown mountain Crow and I'm here to tell you, it had been a battle galore. The way I figured it, if Festus and Bob ever tangled, like grandpa, my money was on Bob.

I had seen that huge Crow drop out of the big blue spruce in front of the woodshed last summer. Grandma had set out some food for old Bob and that big crow had been watching and since he was the biggest bully bird in our neck of the woods, he acted like that food had been expressly delivered for his dining pleasure. But, as if by mutual arrangement, around the corner came old Bob and neither he nor that big crow was going to give up their meal without a fight. And Boy Howdy, talk about a fight!

Archie Matthews

I can't rightly remember who actually got in the first lick, but I can tell you who got in the next several, for that big Crow hopped atop Bob's back and began to play that cats head every bit as good as a woodpecker does the bongo's. The staccato that hard black beak drummed on poor old Bob's noggin sounded like a machine gun ripping off rounds, hard and fast.

And I'll have to admit; I was more than a bit concerned for granddads old tom cat in that particular round of the fight. Poor old Bob let out a loud "Squall" and began to buck and jump as if he were a buck'n bull at a Rodeo and his life depended on either win or end up hamburger. And seeing his poor noggin begin to bleed, I wasn't too sure that "Hamburger" just might be the outcome.

Then Bob stopped running and in mid jump, spun in his skin and was suddenly belly up and had grabbed that massive crows head in his mouth. At the same instant, he surrounded the Crows torso with all four machete lined paws and with one loud "Crunch", the fight was all but over, except for the death throes of flapping wings and flying black feathers.

I remember at the time thinking that Crow was huge in comparison to old Bob, who himself, was no small customer as far as cats are concerned. But it seemed it wasn't the size of the combatant in the fight, as much as the size of the fight in the combatant, that mattered. And nobody could question that old tom cat wasn't a scrapper from a way back, especially after conquering that big Crow.

But I hadn't ever seen Festus in a scrap, other than seen him "Yipe!" and run like a girl with her pig tail pulled, when he'd first met Bob. Oh sure, Mr. Wellner had remarked how Festus was a "Ba'r Dog", but I'd heard him say that about all his dogs. And I had my doubts about what kind of "Ba'r Dogs" his wiener dogs would be, come a face to face encounter with a hungry bear. I imagined them wiener dogs would go down a bear's gullet just as quickly as my dropped hot dog had disappeared in that dog pile last summer. And even as tough as little Festus might act, he wasn't any bigger than a wiener dog, and I imagine to a bear, he'd go down just as smooth, wire hair, stumpy tail and all, with or without ketchup or mustard, just as any hotdog would.

It was a few evenings later, we were setting on the front porch, grandma in her chair knitting, Festus by her side, grandpa in his chair, and I on the large handrail banister that surrounded the porch. Grandpa slowly bent over and picked up an old coffee can that set close to his chair leg and spit a wad of chewing tobacco. He had just set back and was taking another pinch of tobacco from the small round can he kept in his shirt pocket, when grandma looked at me and said, "Best go water your mule before dark."

Confusing though it may be, I didn't rightly have a "Mule" let alone the need to "water one". Grandma always just said that in reference to a fellow going to the bathroom. When I'd asked her why it was called that, she explained it was better than saying "go pee". But when I asked her why she never watered "Her mule"....she gave me that look, and told me to just "Scat and do what I was told."

Grandpa had chuckled and shook his head when I'd asked. I never did get an explanation why men "Watered their mules" and women "Went to the water closet." It was a source of confusion until well into puberty. It seemed every "Male", human or critter was expected to "Water his mule". I, grandpa and even Festus were expected to go off and "water our mule". But grandma, it seems, just visited the "Water Closet"....it wasn't even called an "Outhouse" when a woman visited it. It was referred to as the "Water Closet"....even though there really wasn't any water in the "closet". I still shake my head at the confusion of it, but that's the way it was, or so she assured me.

I was just getting to my feet, when grandma said, "Festus, go water your mule". And Festus jumped to his feet and bolted down the steps on his way to the back yard, and crashed right smack dab into Bob, as he came strolling around the corner of the hedge.

Archie Matthews

Now you talk about an instant fight. I couldn't tell you who had who, for all I could make out was fur a flying and loud ear piercing complaints from both contenders about being so unexpectantly ambushed. Around and around they went in a ball of fury. Grandma began screaming and grandpa started a coughing fit. All I could do was watch as the ball of teeth and claws rolled under the trumpet vine by the front fence.

Talk about a "Ruckus", you'd have thought there was a large pack of hunting dogs with no fewer than six or seven full sized mountain lions a tangling in that bush. I thought that trumpet vine was going to fly apart for all the violent shaking. And then just as quickly as it began, out shot Festus. He ran to the bottom of the steps and whirling around he crouched into his fighting stance and growled, ever hair standing on end, including his stubbed tail.

Then out stepped Bob the big black and white tom cat, as if he didn't have a care in the world, least of which was that feisty little runt of a dog. Bob looked up at us and gave a "Meow" and just walked right up to Festus as if to say, "you want more, I've got plenty more where that came from".

Festus just stood where he was, his legs quivering, his hair and stub tail standing straight up, growling as if he were an eight hundred pound grizzly bear, refusing to give an inch of ground.

We all just sat there frozen waiting to see what was going to happen next. Grandpa had coughed back up the tobacco he'd all but swallowed and grabbing his coffee can spittoon, he spat just as Bob walked up the steps and jumped into his lap. Festus, seeing Bob had claimed grandpa's lap as his own, scampered up and into grandma's lap. And with the boundary lines drawn, each claiming territory to occupy, from that day on it seemed there was a truce, albeit a shaky one.

The days tumbled by as summer days do for a young boy on summer break. And with each passing day both dog and cat

The Stink Eye

soon got used to one another. Oh, I'm not saying there weren't some miner boundary disputes as with any two opposing forces, but as dogs and cats go, they seemed to tolerate one another.

Once in a while Bob would look sideways at Festus and get a growl in return, or Festus would see old Bob with a mouse and would wander a might close for comfort and get the evil eye as Bob would hunch up his back and his hair would stand up. But nary had a fight broke out like the one that threatened to defoliate the trumpet vine.

Then one evening just before twilight grandma sent me off to the outhouse to "Water my mule" before bed. So I traipsed off to the outhouse while Festus was sent to "Water his mule too". I went out the north gate and up the trail to the outhouse and Festus headed around the far side of the woodshed as was his habit, to water his mule somewhere outback.

I was about "mid-water" when I heard Festus start barking. It wasn't his normal scolding bark, but a different kind of bark, more like a playful friendly kind of bark. After completing my "Water 'n the mule" task, I came back into the house and grandma asked what Festus had been barking at. I just shrugged my shoulders and didn't give it much thought. After a few more minutes there was a scratch at the back door and grandma let Festus in.

We should have known then something was up, for the little bugger was dancing around the room wagging his little stump like he'd made a new friend, and although we didn't know it at the time, he had.

The next week, every evening we went about our normal evening routine, we'd eat dinner then spend our evenings out on the front porch, except for Wednesday evenings when I and grandpa's favorite TV show "The High Chaparral" was on, then we'd be in front of the television. But despite where we spent our evening, right after dinner, I'd wander to the outhouse and

Archie Matthews

Festus would run around the woodshed and have the time of his life.

That Wednesday evening grandma had gone out to get a load of clothes off the line and coming back inside, announced "Festus has a little friend."

Since I and grandpa were deeply engrossed watching our favorite western television program. I vaguely remember grandma's announcement somewhere during the "exciting Indian attack" and therefore it came and went without a lot of comment, from either me or grandpa. Later we were to rue that moment of distraction and wish we'd paid more attention to that little tidbit of information.

The next few evenings were spent uneventful out upon the front porch, and grandma got to where she'd tell Festus, "Now go play with your friend." And every evening that little dog would go out back of the wood shed and playfully bark and have a good time, always coming back inside like he'd just had the time of his life. That is until that next evening.

That evening things started off as they usually did. I was off to the outhouse and grandma sent Festus on his way. Once again, having completed my outhouse task and having fulfilled my livestock watering duties, I returned and this time as I entered the house, I heard grandma and grandpa arguing.

Grandpa was scolding grandma for not wearing her glasses. Over the past couple of years, Grandma had gotten pretty near sighted and could hardly see across the room. So a couple of months ago, grandpa had taken her all the way to town, some sixty miles to see the eye Doctor. Evidently as grandpa had predicted, the eye doctor had proscribed grandma eyeglasses. Therefore, upon their return home, grandma sported a pair of glasses, but that didn't seem to correct her seeing problems, for she'd hardly ever wore them.

The Stink Eye

Grandma hated to wear the things, and was always setting them down somewhere and misplacing them. Consequently she still struggled with seeing farther than several feet away. In fact, that very morning she had quite an embarrassing encounter with poor old Ace' Glean the neighbor across the street.

That afternoon grandpa had gotten a little behind his time and forgot lunch time was straight up noon, and grandma having lunch ready, went to see where he was. Grandma arriving out at the gate, saw a blurred image she thought was grandpa and began to mildly berate him for being late to lunch. The blurry looking shape seeming to ignore grandma and her chastisement, just kept walking up the street, by the gate and ignoring grandma and her insistence that "Lunch is ready!"

Poor old Ace' not understanding that grandma was getting as "Blind as a Bat", or so grandpa described it, couldn't understand why his across the street neighbor lady of many years was now screaming at him to "Get his "keaster" inside and eat his already cold lunch....."

I can't say that I blame the man for breaking out into as fast a trot as a man in his upper seventies could manage. Gaining his own gate on the opposite side of the street, Ace immediately headed for his own door as fast as possible. And although I'm not sure, I imagine he double bolted the door once he was inside. (I know if my neighbor lady began acting like a nut shouting at me to come to lunch, I would have).

Just about the time grandma began to open the gate and proceed over to the Glean's house to drag who she thought had been grandpa fleeing for his life, grandpa appeared at her elbow inquiring why she was shouting at and terrorizing poor old Ace'. After several minutes of heated debate between grandma and grandpa, they went across the street and tried to get someone to come to the door. After another several minutes of coaxing poor Ace' to come to the door, grandpa and then grandma explained and apologies were both given and accepted. I of course had taken all this in from peeking out through the screen door. And it

Archie Matthews

was for just this kind reason grandpa was constantly giving her a bad time for not wearing her glasses.

They were thus engaged when I came in and sat down, when Festus began barking and grandpa dropped the eye glass subject for another.

"What's that dog doing out there every night?" grandpa asked. "He's got a friend." Grandma began to explain. "I saw him the other night playing out behind the woodshed with Bob. They're the best of friends now. They are a sight to see, both running around, jumping and playing together. I never did see a dog and cat play so well together."

To this day, those words still ring in my ears, for she no more than got them out, when suddenly we heard Festus's playful bark turn into a mournful wail. Grandma jumped up so fast her knitting was sent clear across the room and landed in the wood box. Gaining her feet, grandma dashed out the back door and opened the porch screen door. Holding the screen door wide grandma began calling out, "Festus, baby.....come to ma' ma!"

It was about that time, that grandpa suddenly sat bolt upright in his recliner and pointed, there lying right under the kitchen table, was Bob, the black and white cat.

"Do you smell that?" he quickly asked and I surely did, for the stench liked to have punched me right in the nose.

"Clara....Shut the door! Shut the door! Clara.....Shut the door!!" grandpa shouted as he struggled to get the foot rest down on his recliner and scrambled to his feet.

But it was too late. In the back door came Festus, like a bullet shot out of a stink gun. He came in the back door just as I and grandpa were clawing and climbing over one another headed out the front door, as the house was instantly permeated with the horrid smell of skunk.

The Stink Eye

Since neither of us had the sense to shut the door behind us, that darn little stink dog came running right out behind us, wailing his head off begging for help.

I had the good sense to head straight out the front gate and slamming it behind me, turned around just in time to see grandpa round the far corner of the house with the evil smelling, stink dog close at his heels.

I could hear grandma still calling "Festus…here Festus!" as she stepped out the front door with her nose firmly pinched. I heard the back door slam shut and saw grandpa making tracks through the house headed for front door, where grandma was still shouting for Festus, and here came grandpa shouting, "Clara, close the door, close the door!"

Long story short, grandpa finally got grandma to shut the doors leaving me and Festus outside. Festus inside the yard and me on the outside, but I was happy to have that fence and gate between us and quickly retreated across the street to the café'. As I approached, the owners, Eddy and his wife Elaine were coming outside to see what all the fuss was about. Eddy no more than made it out and on the step, than he too began to pinch his nose. Elaine stopped on the top of the step, took one good whiff turned right around was back inside and quickly shut the door.

Eddy, looked at me and said, "Well, I guess someone ran into a skunk, from the smell of it."

I nodded, "Festus", I said matter a factly.

Eddy nodded, "When things settle down over there and you get back inside, tell your grandpa, I'll set out a couple big cans of tomato juice by his gate. He'll know what to do with them." And with a chuckle and a shake of his head, Eddy went back inside.

That was as dreary a night as I've ever had as a kid, laying upstairs in bed listening to grandpa's shouting, growling and

Archie Matthews

banging in the woodshed, mixed with the mournful wail of a little dog, all the while grandma's high pitched voice trying to sooth both man and beast. Grandpa and grandma spent most of the night scrubbing the little stink dog, and only well after midnight did the clamor in the woodshed finally die down. But the smell and the memory of it, lasted much longer, in and out of the woodshed.

The next day, despite the late night episode, everyone was up at the crack of dawn as usual. The only difference was there was a lot of evil looks going around at the breakfast table that morning.

Grandma with her bloodshot eyes sat there shooting grandpa an evil look.
"How was I supposed to know that was a skunk and not your black and white tomcat?"

Grandpa with his red rimmed eyes glaring back at grandma, "If you'd been wearing your glasses, you'd have seen the difference between the cat and a skunk!"

And then there was Festus forever nicknamed by me as "The Stinker", sitting over in the corner behind the coal stove on an old towel, every bit as sad and forlorn as Cinderella, shooting everyone an evil look with his squinty eye.
Unless you've ever seen a tomato red, squint eyed, wire haired terrier that smelled as if he'd rolled in a dead skunk, you've never seen a more "Evil Look", from that day forward it's been referred to as, "**The Stink Eye**"!

The Stink Eye

Archie Matthews

The Stink Eye

The Milk Jug Helmet

What young boy hasn't dreamed of being a knight in shining armor? Not the tall broad shouldered, long flowing haired "Dream Boat" girls fantasize about, but a real sword wielding Dragon slayer.

As a young lad of five, I had watched an afternoon Matinee at the local theatre, and instantly knew I was destined to become a Knight in shining armor.

Upon arriving home after the movie, I'd immediately set about making myself a suit of armor. Since it was mid-afternoon dad was still at work, this allowed me time to scrounge in his workshop, which was actually the garage, but dad insisted the portion where his "work bench" was located be called the "Workshop", or so he had informed mom. Dad always frowned at me "borrowing his stuff". But since I had free run of the garage, I immediately went to exploring this pile for useable armor.

Right off I found a bright chrome hub cap. It had a marvelous red and black emblem smack in its center. Upon closer inspection I realized the emblem was a bright red and black outlined bird with a huge wingspread. It was perfect for a breastplate and so with a liberal length of wire, that I found hanging from the work bench, I fixed a loop so that it would hang precisely in front of my chest, with the bird's wings centered perfectly. With my breastplate in place, I began the search for the perfect helmet.

In the movie, every knight had a spectacular helmet that not only protected his head but also had colorful streamers and bangles that enhanced his manly knightliness. But I soon realized a good fitting helmet was extremely hard to come by, let alone one that looked half way decent perched upon my head.

I tried a galvanized bucket, but in placing it on my head, it slipped clear to my shoulders and wobbled around so much, it liked to bash my brains out just trying it on for size. Therefore it was quickly dismissed and I went on searching. I soon found an old orange clay pot that had the dead shriveled remains of an old plant still in the dusty soil, after quickly emptying the old soil out onto the garage floor; I placed it on my head. The pot fit fairly well and I was just about to congratulate myself when I bent over and began to brush the freshly dumped out dirt under dad's workbench where it wouldn't be so noticeable, when I banged my helmet against the leg of the workbench. I will say this for my newfound helmet, it did save me from getting a knot on my head, but upon doing its duty, it immediately fell into several pieces. With a grunt of disgust, I brushed the "helmet" pieces under the

The Milk Jug Helmet

workbench along with the dried up plant and the soil and continued my search for a longer lasting more durable helmet.

I soon found an empty plastic milk jug with the bottom conveniently cut out lying under the work bench. The handle and lid were intact and with a hefty dose of black spray paint that I found setting on the work bench, I quickly had a fantastic black helmet that set off my silver breastplate. Since the handle of the milk jug sat so conveniently towards the back of my head, I tied a red handkerchief to it for a brilliant red streamer, just like one of the knights had worn in the movie. After several minutes of prancing around and looking at my reflection in the shiny surface of an old stainless steel waste basket, I was satisfied I all but fit the bill of a genuine Knight.

Upon realizing I was set in the armor department, I began searching around for a trusty sword. Every boy will tell you the sword is the most important part of a Knight's equipment and I immediately recognized the deep seated need for a "Spectacular Sword". Although I'd used just an old stick in the past, I now realized after watching King Arthur and his knights, I needed something much more battle worthy. Besides, what with my spectacular armor upgrades, now I needed an "Excalibur" and a wooden stick just wouldn't do.

I sorted through dad's tool box and tried several items out that had magnificent handles. I fondled and tested large screw drivers and even a small pry bar that had a well fit plastic handle, but these, although they sported nice hilts, were all far too short for the two handed "Dragon Slayer" I had imagined.

Without finding what I needed in the garage, or the workshop, I soon I wandered into the house. Darting from room to room, I proceeded to do my best to evade detection from the "Queen Mother"; or that's what they called the stately old lady that ran the castle in the movie. (Boy's, even little boys, instinctively know mothers' have a deep seated need to keep young knights "Sword-less". Therefore avoiding detection was paramount especially from the Queen Mother.)

Archie Matthews

After searching the back porch I entered the laundry room and turned up nothing but a couple of old rusty coat hangers and a pile of my dad's smelly old work socks. If Medieval Knights had used chemical warfare, I'd have struck the mother lode with those dirty socks. I briefly imagined running up to a fully armored opponent and opening his visor, thrusting in a stinking sock, slamming the poor fellows' lid closed and backing off to watch him quickly succumb to the noxious vapors. Funny though the thought was, I realized that wouldn't be very chivalrous and turned my attention back to finding an acceptable sword. Thus, proceeding down the hallway, I eventually entered my parent's bedroom and eased the door shut so as not to be interrupted by the dear Queen Mother, should she pass by. Nothing will interrupt a young knights search for a deadly weapon, like the Queen Mother passing by and catching him rifling through her and the Kings bedroom.

I first searched under their bed and found all manner of strange and mysterious items, but nothing that hinted of a sword. Then after searching their closet I turned back towards the door, and there it was. I spied it hidden behind the very door I had just come through. I sped over and my mouth fairly watered at seeing my new "two handed sword". Oh sure, it was still in the rustic shape of my dad's favorite golf putter but I knew I could take care of that.

The custom rubber wrapped handle was a bit worn from the many years of use dear old dad had put it through on the golf course. The once bright silver plated shaft that had been so faithfully buffed and polished after each use was now worn thin in places, and the once bright golden colored head was now a dull bronze. But, needless to say, I immediately recognized its potential and snatching it up snuck out of the house and back to dad's workshop.

First of all, I removed the putter head the quickest way I knew, by prying it back and forth in dad's vise until it snapped off. The now useless hunk of bronze hastily booted beneath the work

The Milk Jug Helmet

bench to join the old potting soil, the shriveled dead plant and what remained of the broken clay pot. I had learned early how to dispose of evidence, as every kid does that wants to keep on living, especially when messing around with their father's treasures.

Then finding a large hammer that just happened to be lying around, I imagined myself as a weapon smith of old, and hammered the silver plated hollow shaft into a flat blade. Oh sure, it sounds easy in the telling, but it's not easy balancing an old golf club in one hand and a huge hammer in the other, while using the top of dads lawn mower as an anvil. Only one in about six hammer blows actually made progress and hit the shaft, while the others ricocheted off various parts of the lawn mower, throwing bits and pieces of the engine here and there. No matter, for they were just as easily scooted out of sight and mind under the bench with either my left foot or the right.

Finally, after what seemed like forever to my worn out arm, not to mention the whittled down lawn mower, I smiled with triumph, and held my mighty two hand sword aloft.

"Perfect!" I all but shouted to myself.

I remember running outside into the yard and declaring war against the huge weeping willow that inhabited the back yard. I charged and flailed away at the hanging branches all the while imagining them as the tentacles of a huge blood thirsty monster. After a bit, having pared down the number of hanging limbs considerably, I raced towards the large tree trunk for the fatal "Coup 'de gra"; But "Alas, t'was not to be", for in raising my sword aloft overhead, I inadvertently smote myself atop my helmet and was instantly blinded.

It took me but an instant to realize my helmet had slid down over my eyes. Being painted black the milk jug helmet was pitch dark and I couldn't see a thing. Therefore, I quickly dropped" Old Dragon Slayer" and began doing my best to pull my helmet back up and uncover my eyes. It didn't take me long to realize I was in

Archie Matthews

trouble for the more I worked trying to get the helmet off, the farther down it slipped. That's when I began to battle my own helmet as if it were the enemy, battle screams and all.

After what seemed like hours of screaming and tugging, I heard mom coming out the back door. "What's all the screaming about?"

I remember her doing her best to calm me as she tried to pull the milk jug off, but it only resulted in even higher pitched screams and my feet left the ground more and more frequently with every one of her increasingly urgent tugs upon the protruding handle.

It didn't take but a few times of being picked up by the helmet and shook, that I ramped up the excitement by declaring, "I can't breathe!"

That's when my contagious panic spread and instantly infected my protective mother bear. The next thing I knew I was being half drug, half carried by my "Milk Jug Helmet Handle" at an ever quickening pace. Any kid will tell you, it's amazingly difficult to keep pace with an adult when you're a short legged child of five, but the difficulty increases exponentially when you are blind and being drug along by your helmet handle, encased head and all.

Where we were headed, I had no idea, what with my feet only briefly and occasionally hitting the ground, I couldn't even tell you which direction or how far we went, what with not being able to see a thing, nor hear anything above my own screaming. I do remember my feet only touched the ground ever so often, my panicked mothers pace increasing it seemed with every one of my muffled wails of terror.

We hadn't gone far before poor mother began screaming and sobbing barreling along like a runaway plow mule dragging the plow. For every time my feet hit the ground they dug in and cut a trench you could have planted potatoes in.

The Milk Jug Helmet

After what seemed like twice the distance of the infamous "Bataan Death March", I heard my father's voice call out from a distance and was quickly answered by mother's frantic scream for "Help!"

Hearing dad, I realized we were running down the half mile stretch of road to the feed mill where he worked. I felt a bit of relief to hear dad's quickly approaching footsteps as he ran up to me and mom. And then just as the panic had ebbed, it once again flowed and overwhelmed me as mom began shouting, "He's suffocating!"

I can only speculate as to the look on dad's face as he quickly assessed the situation, a hub cap dangling from my chest, a black milk jug on my head with a flowing red handkerchief streaming out behind; as sad a bedraggled battle worn knight if ever there was one, and completely devoid of my glorious two handed sword, which had been so casually forgotten in the back yard.

I distinctly remember him shouting to mother, "Frieda! Calm down he's not suffocating, not with that much screaming, he's getting plenty of air."

"For the life of me, I can't pull the milk jug off his head!" mom wailed, "I've pulled and pulled until I've almost pulled his head off!" And with that she demonstrated, as once again I was lifted off the ground by my helmet. I was really beginning to have second thoughts about helmets having handles, for as handy as it might sound in theory, the practicality of it was terribly lacking.

I could feel dad's rough hands exploring around the bottom of the rough cut jug bottom as it was tightly wedged down around my ears and the bottom of my nose, the suction was immense around my sweaty forehead. Then after a few seconds of assessing the situation, I heard dads chuckle, "Well for crying out loud!"

Archie Matthews

And reaching up, he simply unscrewed the milk jug cap thereby releasing the vise like suction around my head as my helmet "Popped off " and my body dropped back to earth from the dangling grip of my mother. I'll never forget the look on her face, standing there holding my black milk jug helmet looking down at me, tears still running down both of our cheeks, yet there dad stood with a huge grin of relief and satisfaction on his face.

I won't bore you by describing the harried return trip back home or the diminishing laughter from my father as he returned to work. No need to go into the excruciating detail of being chased all the way home by an angry woman with a black milk jug in hand, all the while grumbling she's lost ten years of her life.

Oh, and as far as I know, the local police never did catch the vandal or vandals that broke into dads' garage and pummeled his old lawn mower into pieces with his own hammer. The local law enforcement said they'd never seen anything so despicable as someone breaking into a man's garage and beating the hell out of his lawnmower. It seems it's forever to remain, a cold case.

One good thing came of that little incident though; dad got the old lawn mower replaced with a brand new one. Of course the whole incident was an enormous puzzlement to dad's insurance company as well, but as the insurance man said, "The worlds full of nuts now days, that'll take any chance they can to wreak vengeance on someone, did you upset someone with your mowing lately?"

Both mom and dad were just as puzzled as the local sheriff and the insurance man, and since nobody ever asked me what I suspected, I just kept my mouth shut and tried to look as innocent as I could.

I will say this, after all the excitement of the "Helmet episode" as it's still referred to; It paled in comparison to the "Mangled Golf Club Incident" that quickly unfolded the following week as dad discovered his favorite putter hidden in the grass with his brand

The Milk Jug Helmet

new lawn mower. And what a shame, for I had gone to a lot of work and trouble to make "Old Dragon Slayer" into the sword it was.

Let's just say, the "Sparks flew, during and afterwards"; for it suddenly seemed when dad's new lawnmower met up with his golf club, he began to suspect the vandalizing of his lawnmower and golf club might have been an inside job. Of course it didn't help my case much, when about that same time, mom exited the garage, carrying a waste can of mower, golf club and flower pot parts she'd found under his work bench.

Maybe the case wasn't as cold as I'd hoped.

Archie Matthews

The Milk Jug Helmet

THE GUNFIGHT

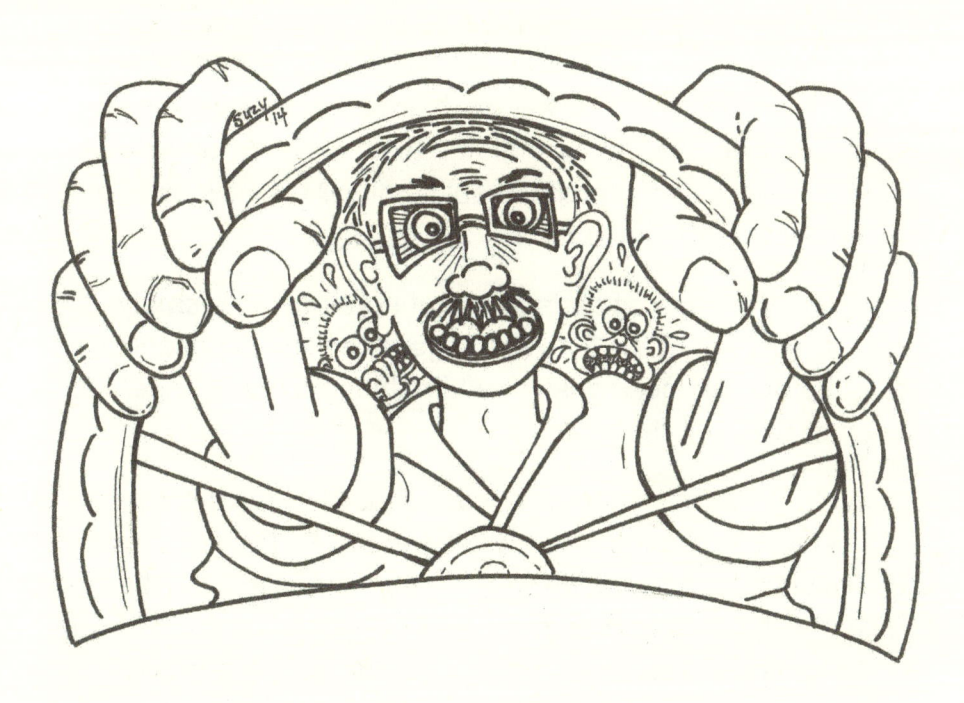

When I was seven I had the ride of my life one summer headed to my grandparent's house in central Idaho. Little did I know what peril I and my family would endure on that four hour drive from our home in Grandview, to Ola, Idaho. Needless to say, it was a long trip, but it was the last several miles of the journey that taxed us the most. It was just down the road from our destination that a fit of road rage ended in the strangest "Gunfight" imaginable.

A few things you must keep in mind while reading this tale of mine. My father was an accomplished sniper in the Korean War and the most magnificent rifle shot I've ever seen in my life. Many was the time growing up and going on hunting adventures together, I've seen him make spectacular shots. I'm not talking about "one shot wonders", but consistent remarkable shots of long distance as well as close range with incredible accuracy and timing, all while keeping a calm and peaceful demeanor.

Another thing you should take into account was dear old dad as a young man had a terrible temper. And as often happens with men that have anger management issues, once my dad lost his temper, he would act like a man possessed. Usually dad was kind, calm and far from hotheaded, but then something would offend his sense of honor or threaten his family. When either of these happened, dad's temper would ignite like a powder keg, and "Boy howdy Watch out!"

Then came the day that dads sense of honor and the safety of his family was put to the test and anger like I've never seen him display before or since consumed him during a brief dangerous encounter while on the road.

I discovered something about my dad that day. Oh, I knew he could get angry, like the time my brother turned the pump on by accident while dad had been working on it and almost lost a couple of fingers. And then there had been the time he'd caught us kids lighting fire crackers while using the vent cap on his underground gas tank to hold them while we put the match to fuse.

But my most startling realization being, how a man that's so good with a rifle, can be so inept with a pistol while in a fit of rage.

But you decide for yourself.

I had once again survived another year of school and like the rest of my class, was paroled for the summer. As in years past, I looked forward to a long leisure summer with my grandparents in Ola, Idaho.

After traveling a long three hours into a four hour trip, we were entering the final leg of our journey to my grandparent's house. I

The Gunfight

distinctly remember the ride up the long meandering valley past the little town of "Sweet" and on up towards the town of Ola. The path we traveled was a narrow two lane paved road with a steep drop off on the one side down to the creek far below. The other side rose from side hill pastures into foot hills and eventually to the mountain tops of the Seven Devil mountains.

The reason I distinctly remember the ride up that summer, was it would be my first encounter with "Road Rage". Back then, road rage wasn't as prevalent as it has become now days. I suppose for years people were still just happy as the dickens to be riding in cars and not atop a horse, or in a drafty old wagon. While now days "Road Rage" is rampant. I guess the sign of a world that no longer appreciates the little things, but is now engrossed in just getting places as fast as they can and woe betide anyone that slows them down or happens to get in the way.

Dad was driving as he often did and mom was sitting in the front passenger seat holding my baby brother Roy who was all of six months old. I and my younger brother Ike sat in the back seat of the old four door car. My youngest brother Nate wasn't even a glint in my folk's eyes yet, so there was just the five of us then, Nate wouldn't come along for another three years. (Although he missed this adventure, he would partake in many others with us later in life....both the good and the bad.)

We were ambling along doing the speed limit on the twisting turning road. Most of the straight stretches you could do a top speed of fifty miles an hour, but most of the time it was between thirty five and forty miles per hour to stay on the safe side. (The safe side, being up on the road and not down in the crick.)

The first sign of trouble was when dad slowed the car down dramatically as we encountered an old truck creeping along with a flatbed full of hay. The hay bales were loosely stacked and must have been recently loaded, for hay dust blew thick off the truck and all but obscured our view of the pickup.

Dad patiently followed behind awaiting a long straight stretch in the road where he could see far enough ahead so that we could pass. The passenger side of our car was facing the long downhill side that quickly dropped off towards the distant creek at the bottom; the driver side of the car being the side that climbed up past a broad expanse of pastures to the foothills and the mountains above.

After several miles of waiting and watching for his opportunity, dad signaled and passed the slow moving truck and once we'd passed he began to pick up speed once again. Then several moments later, I heard dad's loud exclamation and saw the hay truck pull alongside our car and slowly creep inexorably closer and closer edging us towards the embankment drop off. Dad tried to speed up but due to the rough road and the turns didn't dare try to outrun the old truck for fear of either crashing on a turn, or going off the road and plummeting to the creek below. Therefore he did the only other thing he could do and slowed down, but this seemed only to embolden the truck driver, who was bent on edging us over the side of the road and sending us to a watery death far below.

Dad again sped up, only to have the truck speed up and keep pace, then dad rolled his window down and began shouting at the old fellow driving the truck. That's when I noticed the truck driver was an old thin faced fellow with a white stubble beard, wild eyes overhung with huge bushy eyebrows and what looked to be at least three old crooked black teeth. I could see his teeth quite plain, for his mouth was wide open and he was laughing as if he was a kid on his first merry go round ride having the time of his life.

Back and forth he and dad drove, first one edging forward then the other, but always staying close enough that neither could get in front or behind the other. It was only after a couple of harrowing miles like this that my mother's groans of concern blossomed into full fledge screaming and little brother Roy quickly followed suit. I was just astounded that the little old man seemed to be having an absolute blast, while my dad was cussing like a sailor and my mother was screaming as if the world was about to an end.

Then dad seemed to snap and shouted for my mother to "Take the wheel!", and with that, he began to climb out the window towards the truck and its merry driver. My setting in the back seat, and dad being in the front seat, didn't give me an opportunity to see his face, but from his body language and the four lettered words streaming back in my rear door window, I gathered dad's face wasn't as merry as the little old man's.

I'd seen dad mad more than once, in fact, many more times than my backside had ever wished. Dad wasn't a man to throw curses around like some kind of gypsy, or the proverbial sailor. When dad let words fly like he was doing now, he was hot under the collar, and why not, this old devil was doing his utmost to drive dad and his beloved family over the edge and seemed to be getting a kick out of doing it.

The little old man seeing his adversary climbing out the window trying his best to board his truck, seemed to glean even more merriment and began bouncing up and down in his seat, slapping the steering wheel of his truck with both hands. The effect this had on dad was instant and seemed to instill in him

Archie Matthews

some kind of super human strength, or the very least, the semblance of super human strength, for dad grabbed the large mirror of the truck and began doing his best to pull the two vehicles close.

To say pandemonium was loose in our vehicle would have been to say the least, for mother began screaming in even higher pitches and increased volume, as she grabbed the steering wheel that dad had so quickly abandoned. Baby Roy not wanting to come in last place at the screaming contest opened up his lung reserves and bellowed forth his own high pitched screams as mom wrestled with the steering wheel with one hand and dangled him with the other. And sure enough, it wasn't long before the screaming competition in the front seat quickly spilled over into the back seat and younger brother Ike, who up until now had been wide eyed and quiet like me, opened up and joined the choir. I'll never forget how his wee tenor voice hit all the high notes as well as the low notes with every terrifying mile. It was almost like attending some kind of hillbilly motorized opera, what with dad's baritone curses, mom's high pitched aria's and Ike and his loud wavy tenor screams of terror.

At the time it seemed like miles and miles and hours upon hours of harrowing back and forth, side by side death defying driving by my mother and the laughing lunatic in his vehicle. While dad clawed at the side of the fellow's truck screaming how he was going to disassemble the fellow the minute he laid hands upon him, in intimate gruesome detail.

To this day, I'm not sure whether it was the gory detailed description dad was painting for the old fart, or the high pitched screaming reverberating inside our racing car just inches from the dire drop off to a watery death, and for a brief instant, I considered joining the opera singers. But as chance would have

The Gunfight

it, I couldn't quite decide whether to join dad and start raging out my window at the crazed pickup driver, or sit and bellow out death dirges with the women and children. Therefore I just remained wide eyed and quiet with my hair standing straight up.

I suppose had it been anyone other than the laughing lunatic, he might have been concerned, for dad wasn't a man to be trifled with. He was six foot, two hundred and thirty pounds and in top physical shape for a man in his early thirties and although I couldn't see his face, I'd seen his angry face from time to time and knew it was nothing to laugh at. Or should I say, it never struck a smile to my face, let alone laughter, that's when I knew we were dealing with someone way short of a full deck.

And then with a loud crash of metal, dad tore off the large passenger mirror from the truck and began pounding away at the side of the old man's vehicle. Seeing his mirror ripped away only heightened the old fellows' maniacal laughter and his bouncing up and down, and then as if things weren't bad enough, the old gray haired loon began making faces at dad through the passenger window.

As exuberant as the old madman had become, dad's anger instantly ramped up as he bashed in the passenger window with the mirror. Then with a huge one arm heave, he threw the mirror at the old fellow within. All I can say is this, that old fart was either lucky or smart enough to keep that truck just far enough away, that dad couldn't get a good hold to allow him to cross into the old man's vehicle, or things might have turned out entirely different.

As the mirror hit the old fellow aside the head, it must have jarred his " loose wire" back into place for a second or two, for he stopped laughing and got a serious look in his eye. Dad instantly

Archie Matthews

recognized the change and he quickly slipped back down into his seat and began driving intently.

Once again back and forth first our car would gain the lead and then suddenly the old flatbed truck would pull ahead slightly, with one difference now. The old fellow having lost all humor once again began intently nudging our car closer and closer to the edge of the road and the steep drop off.

Then, dad did something that puzzles me to this day. He began to throw things out of our car into the old fellow's truck. First it was an old coffee cup that set up on the dashboard, and without waiting to see the results, he quickly grabbed anything and everything and sent it in the direction of the old man's head in the truck beside us.

At the time, I didn't have the good sense to call out to dad the effects his well-aimed throws were having. I do remember thinking, my dad had an amazing side arm throw and pretty darn good aim at that, for the coffee mug hit and ricocheted off the old fellows temple and made him swerve clear over to the far side of the road. The resulting gap between the vehicles presented dad with an even better angle at his target and his next fusillade, being a heavy metal flashlight, missed the old fellow by a few inches, as it sailed right by his nose and shattered his other door window.

I'm not sure if it was dad's willingness to throw his valuable items at the old fellow or his spectacular aim that impressed the old devil, but right off I noticed the old boy's attitude changed again. Now the laughing maniac seemed to realize dad wasn't to be toyed with and instead of being the aggressor, now switched into flee mode. He suddenly began doing his best to get away from the flying battery of well thrown junk dad was barraging him with.

The Gunfight

No longer did he crowd us towards the steep drop off, but he stayed over in the far lane and concentrated on out running the salvo of hard objects dad sent express air delivery towards his head.

Next was mom's coffee cup, followed by the Hula girl off the dash, her hips still swinging and her grass skirt up around her ears as she sailed over and through the fellow's window. I will never forget how she stuck to the side of his head for the briefest of instants before slowly sliding to his shoulder and perching there for a second as if whispering in his ear. I can't imagine what she might have said, but whatever it was; the little old fellow hunched forward over the steering wheel and gave that old truck everything it had.

With one hand driving and his eyes locked intently forward on the road, Dad's remaining right hand was flying over the top of the dashboard searching for anything to use as ammunition for his one arm catapult. And then finding a full box of pistol shells that he had brought along to do some target practice with grandpa, dad began pelting the old fellow aside the head with the hard little projectiles, one by one. It's amazing how hard those little chunks of lead and steel casing seemed to be, for as they bounced off the old man's noggin, they ricocheted around in his cab making little chips on his front windshield and breaking out the glass instrument panel and gauges.

To this day, I am amazed one didn't go off and kill someone, mainly the old fart with the death wish, but they didn't, they just ricocheted around the cab, with more than a few sailing out either one busted window or the other. I remember seeing the bright polished casings glinting in the sun as they went by my window and fell to the roadway far behind.

Archie Matthews

I often wonder if anyone ever stumbled onto all those unfired shells and question how they came to be strewn along a good half mile of country roadway out in the middle of nowhere. Normally you find "spent or fired" shell casings, but hardly ever unfired cartridges, especially that many spread out over such a distance. I imagine it puzzled the dickens out of someone, I know it still does me and I was there.

As with the initial coffee cup, each shell slammed into the old fellow's temple and I could see his head recoil from the impact as dad fired those shells out faster than any automatic firearm ever could. The old truck sped up and try as he might, the old lunatic couldn't escape the barrage dad was letting fly. Then as the shells ran out, dad's hand once again frantically searched for anything in which to load into his one armed assault rifle.

Quickly opening the glove box, he began grabbing anything of any weight and substance within. I saw him grab a large hunting knife still in the sheath, and lifting it up he shook it at the old man as if to let him know it was coming, and once again let fly. The knife, still in its sheath nearly got the old fellow, but at the last moment the old boy's head leaned back and the knife breezed by his nose and out the window.

I remember a giggle escaped me at the realization of the irony that dad had run out of bullets and the battle had instantly went from a gun fight to a knife fight in short order, without even a gun.

Evidently seeing a fully sheathed knife shown and then thrown at him, once again seemed to tickle the crazed fellows funny bone and again he began laughing and laughing, all the while bouncing on his seat. This renewed hilarity from the mad man only added even more fuel upon dad's fired up rage, as if that was possible and he began an even more desperate search for something to throw.

Seeing dear old dad, our protector and glorious leader in need of ammunition, I did the only thing one compatriot could do for another and I began handing dad all kinds of things from the back seat to throw. First to go were a pair of mom's high heels that happened to be lying on the floor board. Although mom howled upon recognizing her coveted shoes, dad had them aimed, and fired into the old fellows' truck before she could snatch them away.

Seeing dads' effectiveness with foot wear, I quickly realized I had four more close at hand. Ike's went first of course, right off his squirming feet, his loud siren never letting up for a moment, and then both of my cowboy boots went into dads arsenal and out the window, with uncanny accuracy. Those four shoes were still bouncing around the cab of the truck after careening off the old fellows' head, when I realized mom was screaming for me to stop handing dad stuff.

Talk about being instantly scandalized! Here we were under attack by an unknown and unprovoked assailant, dad defending us with everything he had, and mom instructing me to stop aiding the bombardment of our hated enemy by drying up the ammunition supply. I'm sorry to say, I took it rather hard and remember thinking of mother as the next dreaded Benedict Arnold and shot her a disgusted look.

But as with most things, when my mother insist I stop doing something, I capitulated and quickly. Well…. not too quickly, for I had one more item in my left hand, and quickly thrust it over dads left shoulder, thinking mom wouldn't see. Dad once again

Archie Matthews

held the item up and shook it for the laughing old fellow to see before he cocked his arm back for a throw.

A moment before, I had been searching all around the back seat and floor for anything of any weight to throw and had been trying to supply dad with projectiles as quickly as he could rapidly fire out the window at our attacker. I hadn't realized I'd reached up under dad's seat, nor paid attention to what I had handed him, that is until I saw him shake it and cock his arm for the final throw. That must have been the same instant that mom also realized what it was dad was waving and about to let fly out the window. And with one loud "NO!" she grabbed his arm and mutiny broke out in the front seat as well as the back.

What with everyone else howling, now was the time I cut loose and put in my two cents worth, and joining the crowd, I began to shout at dad too. "Dad, stop, don't throw it!" I shouted as mom clutched his arm tightly and began trying to calm the raging storm that happened to be maniacally piloting our vehicle.

I can only surmise from the instant reaction of the truck and its loony occupant, that the laughing old man suddenly realized what dad had waved and now held in his hand. For as quickly as it began, it was over, and the truck violently swerved, careened around a tight corner up on two wheels and down a side road, leaving us alone on the main road to watch its dusty trail quickly disappear far behind us.

Mom and dad continued to struggle for a moment as dad eventually slowed the car to a stop. After checking in the rear view mirror and then again over his shoulder and assured the truck and its crazed driver were gone, his head swiveled around and his mouth gapped open as he realized what he and mom were struggling with.

The Gunfight

There in his hand, held by the barrel, was the pistol we'd all forgotten was under his seat. The very one that my frantic search had produced and been handed over his shoulder to be used as another missile. Neither, I or dad realizing what was about to go out the window. Only upon holding it up and shaking it, showing the old man another object was destined for the side of his already sore head, his arm cocking back ready to send his best weapon out the window in the least efficient manner possible, did both I and mom realize what was about to happen.

Needless to say, it took several minutes for everyone to calm down, especially dad. Mom regained control of baby Roy's volume control and got him turned down to a low whine. While I coaxed little brother Ike into realizing we were not all going to die a horrible death in the creek bottom as he'd been predicting vehemently the past several miles at the top of his lungs.

Only after dad had circled the car a dozen times, smoked two packs of cigarettes, and with the occupants of our car settled down, we proceeded on to grandma and grandpa's house.

At the time, as you can well imagine, it had been no laughing matter. What had incited that old fellow to drive like that and act in such a crazy manner has often been a topic of discussion in our family over the years.

Mom's theory is the old man must have encountered someone with a car like ours previously that had tried to run him off the road and he was merely trying to return the favor.

Dad's theories lean more towards lunacy and genetic instability, what with his being born in that part of the county and having knowledge that some of the locals in that area were just born "a bit off". (It's usually at this part of our discussion that everyone is extremely careful not to mention dad's throwing everything out

Archie Matthews

the window, including a full box of bullets, and nearly the gun itself.)

Whatever the case may be, when our family gets together and we tell our stories around the bonfire, one of my favorite tales to tell is about the "Gunfight", when; "Dad fended off the maniacal little old man having a fit of road rage, by pulling a gun, using a full box of shells, without even a shot fired."

Well, almost in that order.......

The Gunfight

The Dragline

As a kid growing up, I had the fantastic fortune to have spent many a summer with my loving grandparents in Ola, Idaho. At the age of ten, my brother Ike and two of my cousins discovered that summer, the adventures of riding machinery. Not the regular kind of machinery most kids envision today, not the typical tractor or such, but back then, there was a whole different kind of machinery being used, let alone ridden. This is our story of that summer's wild rides on a couple "different kinds" of machinery.

Ace' Glean was the local cattle rancher. He was my granddads age, well into his seventies and by normal standards should have been retired. The men around that part of the country, although old enough to retire, seldom slowed down long enough to notice they'd reached the benchmark, let alone actually slow down and retire.

Ace' and his wife lived in a big house on the opposite side of Main Street from my grandparents. Yet they also had many acres of land that surrounded the small town, one of which was a huge pasture behind their house and across the main road that ran up the long narrow valley. This pasture also lay between the town and the distant "Squaw Crick" that provided all of us kids fishing and swimming adventures to enjoy throughout summer. The biggest problem with that pasture was the compromised access across it when trying to access that crick. This pasture was where Ace' usually kept at least a couple if not several wild range bulls. Also in the very middle of this large pasture, was Ace's huge barn.

Ace's barn was the epitome of huge red and white barns that used to dot the countryside all across America, but have become increasingly scarcer with each decade. This barn was a huge two story affair, with the bottom area having a large central area and the surrounding lower level sported many smaller gated pens designed to hold livestock throughout the winter. This giant structure as so many like it also sported a huge open loft area. Most loft area's held hay in one way shape or form, either loose hay or baled and had some means incorporated into its structure of letting hay down into the pens below. This particular barn had large wooden panels that could be added or removed from the floor giving access to the lower main floor of the barn.

Like many other cattle ranchers Ace kept his hay loose hay in the big loft in the top of his barn. And to get the hay from the wagon far below, he used a large contraption called the "Jackson Fork".

The Jackson Fork was a large wooden implement that had long wooden "Teeth" like a regular fork, that tilted with a set of pulleys tripped by a large handle that once the hay was within and atop the "teeth", the large handle could be tripped and the fork tilted

The Dragline

back to hold the hay inside. Then with a long series of ropes and pulleys, the whole heavy pile of hay and machinery could be lifted up into the loft and pulled inside along a long steel rail suspended from the roof's ridge pole. The hay would then be slid along inside to the far back of the barn and the hay deposited and piled from the back to the front.

As I mentioned the Jackson Fork was attached to a steel rail that lay along the huge beam that protruded out of the loft and could be lowered and raised hauling hay from below to the high loft.

Although it was a bit of a challenge just getting to Ace's barn, since he kept several huge bulls in that particular pasture, us kids thought it was worth the risk of getting gored or trampled to death, to gain the loft and swing way out into space on the Jackson fork and back to the loft. We also enjoyed frolicking in the loose hay and would revel in carrying stones in our pockets to toss down atop a bull as it snorted and pawed below.

Upon gaining the barn, after running the gauntlet of bulls, we would enter through either the big double hung front doors or the big double hung back doors, depending on where we ended up after crossing the field, usually with one or more bulls following close behind. Once safely inside we would make our way up the interior ladder to the loft.

Usually the Jackson Fork was tied off just within the loft doors, sometimes the loft doors would be opened and other times closed. But always the Fork was tied off with the end of the rope to a large steel cleat just inside the door opening. Depending upon how the Fork was tied off and which particular end of the rope was used, depended on whether or not it went up and down, or just slid way out to the outside end of the rail and back.

We always tied off the up/down rope so that the Fork only slid out and not down to the ground, this allowed a kid to set in the rake and be pushed out to the far end of the rail, far above the ground below. Reaching the end, the Fork would swing and twirl and then someone remaining in the loft would pull the rope and the Fork back inside to exchange riders.

Then one day, my cousin Micky Hervle rode the Fork, but we had mistakenly forgotten to tie the pulley line off solid so it wouldn't slide down the rope. Poor Micky had learned three hard lessons that day. The first of course being you have to make sure a large implement that slides on a pulley is tied off, if you don't want to ride it to the end of the rope. The second lesson being, if you're the one at risk of dying, you should be the one doing the tying to make sure it's done right. The third lesson of course, was just how hard the ground was that time of year after a thirty foot drop.

This was the same summer that my brother Ike ,age 8 and our cousin Dean also age 8 and Micky age 9 and just a year younger than I was, had all jointly spent the summer with our grandparents.

As was our habit, we had drawn straws to see who was first and second and so forth. That day poor Micky was unfortunately the first to ride the fork. Upon arriving in the loft, Micky had immediately boarded the Fork and shouted. "Push me out!" And we did, but, and this being the unfortunate part, no one had thought to check the up/down pulley rope was properly tied off. The minute the Fork, with Micky aboard was pushed out the loft door, pulleys whirled and ropes smoked as the farm machinery implement sped at break neck speed to the earth below.

"Below" meaning ground level and from the sound of the impact of his body hitting the dirt, it was hard ground. Neither Fork, nor Micky had bounced, but instead had just "sickenly smacked" into the ground, both laying there in pieces. One difference between the pieces being, Micky was making loud ear piercing sounds, while the Fork wasn't making any sound now at all. And probably a good thing, for Micky's screaming scared the bulls, and had sent them off running towards the distant crick, clearing a path for us, ("Us" being the survivors able to move our limbs.) to leave the barn and run to town to seek help.

Due to the inability of Micky to move any of his limbs in a normal fashion, that and the odd angle that his arm bent and his collar bone twisted his body at that funny angle, we knew he wasn't going to be able to run for help, himself.

Upon alerting grandma to Micky's plight, and returning with her in tow, all it took was one quick look from grandma to know Micky needed more than a Band-Aid or a splash of Mercurochrome to cure. Therefore she had sent me back to Eddy Mehan's café to use the only phone in town to call Mr. Wellner's daughter Joyce. Joyce happened to live down the crick a ways and was a registered nurse. She had come driving up in her large station wagon with the bright red cross painted on the front doors. After a few minutes of inspection, she announced Micky had a couple bones broken and away they went towards the distant town of Emmett, some seventy miles away, siren blaring.

Meanwhile, the rest of our adventurous group was marched back to town at the end of a smartly snapping willow switch deftly wielded by the cranky little old woman, we fondly called grandma. Of course the "Fondly" was usually when she didn't have the willow switch snapping at our backsides.

Herding us back into town, she quickly drove us towards grandpa's blacksmith shop and we instantly realized we were in for a good tongue lashing as well as the willow switching we were now receiving.

Nobody on earth, my mother included, could give a young lad a tongue lashing and dressing down, like dear old grandpa. He

Archie Matthews

was a marvel at it and with just a handful of well combined words, could make even a "smart-alec-kid" feel like he was about two inches tall. I'd have far rather been switched a dozen times over than be tongue lashed by grandpa. But here we were and here it came.

We were herded into the shop and grandpa seeing us high step'n it before grandma just inches in front of the snapping willow switch, eased over to his flaming blacksmith forge and shutting his blower off, he raked some coal to stoke the fire and sat down on his nail keg.

We were lined up like criminals facing the judge as grandma laid out the prosecutor's version of what had transpired. I have to say, for not even being present at the actual crash, she did outline the events pretty close to accurate. All expect for the part where "Poor little Micky had been finagled into riding the Fork and all the while not even knowing any better."

I took exception to that, for grandma was always claiming we put Micky up to things that he didn't know any better. That was a misconception and far from the truth and I was never want for lack of arguing the point, but wasn't about to with a woman holding a switch, let alone a cranky grandma. So we did what we did best in these types of instances, and we just stood with heads bowed in deepest shame, and bobbed or shook our heads in the appropriate directions to fit the questions.

The only time we weren't in unison was when grandpa suggested that it might just have been "MY" idea since I was the oldest and thereby labeled the "Ring Leader". My head was the odd man out and nodded in the "NO" direction, while my loving brother and his evil henchman Dean, both decided to throw me under the proverbial Jacks Fork and sacrifice me to save themselves.

The Dragline

Their resulting treachery was thereby rewarded by escaping with just a minor tongue lashing and early release for time served and "snitching". The evil little rats, they would get theirs, and oh how I was going to make them pay, but at that time none of us understood how dire their payback almost became.

After grandma marched the reprieved twosome off, leaving me alone with grandpa, that's when I really got the talking too. Grandpa wanted to hear the whole story, which I told to the best of my ability without any blemish or garnishment.

I told how we had dodged bulls, gained the barn climbed to the loft and launched Micky out the loft doors and how he mistakenly crashed to the ground. The whole time grandpa listened intently, trying his best to not fall off his nail keg every time we came to a life or death decision moment. Then after hearing the ambulance part and that Micky was headed back to Emmett to get bandaged up, grandpa said, "Come on, we need to go call his mother and let her know her baby boy is headed her way."

I remember grandpa shaking his head and looking a little older and grayer around the edges and we trudged out of the shop and across the road to the gas station/café to use the pay phone.

Grandpa dug around in his pocket and came up with change and depositing several coins he dialed several numbers. It wasn't long before grandpa began explaining to Aunt Nell that her youngest boy was on his way back to the town they lived in to have some bones put back in place. I remember the screeching on the other end of the line and grandpa holding the phone out at arm's length until the wailing lowered in both pitch and volume. After a few minutes grandpa nodded this way and that and then said "Goodbye" and hung up the phone.

"Well, I'd say she took that about as expected. Needless to say, Micky probably won't be coming back to spend the summer." He

Archie Matthews

said a bit sadly and then he smiled. "It's time you headed back to the house, I got work to do. Tell your grandma I called Nell and if I was you, I'd take my time getting there. Better to give your grandma some time to cool off." And with that, he went back to the shop and I meandered my way to the house.

Several days later in the middle of the afternoon, we were all surprised to see Aunt Nell and Uncle John come pulling up to the house in their big truck with Micky in tow. We had all been sitting on the front porch after finishing up our lunch of Spam sandwiches.

If you've eaten Spam, you'll know what I'm talking about, but for those that don't, let's just say, it was "Canned Meat". I never did know what kind of meat, and quite frankly, was smart enough to never ask. From the looks of it, it was a conglomeration of every kind of cast off part of every kind of critter imaginable. All squished into a can with some kind of gelatin to fill the creases and cracks, both in the can, and in your innards as it was consumed.

I never did understand why my grandmother used the stuff, for grandpa was a magnificent hunter, not to mention fisherman and even if he hadn't been, we could have eaten road kill that I'm sure would have tasted better. Needless to say, it was eat it or complain about it and get it shoved down my gullet at the end of a willow switch liberally applied to my backside. Although I wrinkled my nose at the sight of the stuff, I was smart enough to stuff it in and gulp it down as quickly as I could, trying my best to not even taste the vile stuff. The only time it got even worse, was when grandma got a wild hair and fried the stuff in a skillet. You can choke down raw squishy Spam fast, but once it's got that hard fried crust, you definitely have to chew and chew and chew the stuff.

The Dragline

My grandpa said bear meat in his opinion was the worst meat a man could eat. He claimed a bite sized piece of bear meat would grow every time you bit down on it, until it had to be spit out it was so big and vile. I imagine Spam must have contained a lot of bear meat, if not worse.

Upon seeing their only daughter arrive, grandma and grandpa were elated and there were smiles all around as Aunt Nell and Uncle John came up the walkway, leading poor bandaged, hobbling Micky. After gaining the porch everyone was seated, including bent little Micky being lifted up by his father and placed in a huge wooden armchair. That's when I noticed Micky had one boot that was six times larger than his other boot.

In answer to grandma's inquiry Aunt Nell began to describe Micky's condition. It seems he had broken his arm and collar bone, not to mention a finger or two. He wore his left arm in a cast and it was tied close to his chest with what appeared to be an old diaper, but nobody kidded him about that and seemingly tried not to notice that it was actually a diaper. A couple of his fingers were all wrapped up with a couple of splints that looked like popsicle sticks and white tape. He also wore a weird metal contraption called a "back brace" that was supposed to help keep his collarbone where it should be.

Grandma and grandpa both "ewe'd and awed" over the bandages and then grandpa remarked about the size of that monster boot on one foot. It seems that Micky also suffered a couple broken toes on his right foot, which was a bit remarkable since all his other broken pieces were located on his left side, but I guess I was the only one to notice that odd detail.

Anyways, Uncle John explained it was one of his old logging boots and Micky wore it, and three pair of heavy wool socks underneath for protection for those busted toes. He also remarked the doctor had taped them toes together, but there

Archie Matthews

wasn't much else they could do with them, other than protect them the best they could, hence the giant steel toed boot.

After hearing about all the doctoring and the bandaging and listening to both Aunt Nell and Uncle John bemoan how much "That was going to cost them."

Aunt Nell explained that Micky had claimed all responsibility for the rash adventure and had even told how he had heroically fought the rest of us back so that he could take the first and riskiest ride.

I thought for a minute I was about to puke as all the adults smiled at poor Micky's bravery and honest admission that he had been the instigator, and how they were all so proud of him owning up to his mistake. I looked over at both Ike and Dean and seen they too were experiencing the same disgust that I was, that or their bellies were still wrestling with those spam sandwiches we'd all had to eat, it was hard to tell which was more upsetting at that moment.

Aunt Nell went on to explain that Micky had put up such a fuss about not being able to come back and spend the summer that they just couldn't punish him by keeping him home. Not after all his honest exaltations, not to mention all his promises of "from now on trying to set a good example for the rest of us to follow". Once again I felt my spam sandwich trying its best to make a break for it back up the way it went down, and only with enormous self-control did I keep it down after hearing such disgusting talk.

Soon, and as far as I was concerned, just in the nick of time, us kids were told to go and play and off we went, with Micky hobbling close behind. Of course what with that boot being about six sizes too big for him, it slowed him down considerably

The Dragline

as he'd half drag it and half lift the enormous thing trying to make any headway he could.

We ambled around the back yard and explored the back of the woodshed. Being all boys, we quickly engaged in one of our many competitive sports, one of which was seeing who could pee the highest up the back of the woodshed. (Authors note; girls, should quickly skip down past this paragraph, this doesn't concern you.), but lads, take heed, all boys know this game, each and everyone one of you reading.

As boys will be boys, each and every one that came to spend any time with grandma and grandpa knew of the back of the woodshed and the chalk marks there on that back wall. Whether family, relative or just visiting male acquaintance, everyone knew that we kept track of who could pee how high. The entire back of the woodshed had varying chalk marks that stretched back to the eons of time. I can't swear by it, but I even seem to remember such names as Daniel Boone and Davy Crockett etched somewhere on the back of that woodshed. Needless to say it was where the young men congregated to compare each one's ability in making the highest mark.

Now this being a family type story, I am not going to go into the intimate details of how this individual or that each had their own method of achieving height. Let's just say, every guy was different and no two individuals were quite the same and leave it at that.

The rules were very simple, each in turn stepped up and did his best to mark as high on the wall as physically possible. All kinds of stances and tactics were deemed fair, the only rule that remained firm, was you couldn't stand on anything. It was this well-known rule that at that moment became a hot topic of debate. It started with Dean realizing as Micky was standing at the wall preparing to take his turn that he was putting his weight, and height, all upon the giant boot. This was evident by his other, normal sized shoe being raised up and off the ground almost two inches, while as Dean so hotly pointed out, Micky gained an unnatural advantage. Micky instantly took umbrage at the fact he was accused of "Cheating", while Dean became instantly scandalized as my brother Ike pointed out, since Dean never could achieve any significant height, the argument was a "Moot Point". This being pointed out set the entire group into a yelling fit that threatened to bring the adults and nobody want that so a quick compromise was agreed upon.

I pointed out that since Micky's original shoe hung two inches off the ground, we would measure that with a stick and then subtract that from the top of his mark. There was a brief misunderstanding about just what was going to be measured with a stick and subtracted, but after a few minutes of clarification and almost laughing my guts out at the mix up, we proceeded with the contest.

I am not at liberty to disclose the winner nor loser of this competition, for the rules of conduct that surround this event strictly limit the individual outcomes to be officially marked on the woodshed back wall and can only be referred to by actual qualified participants. We do that to protect the innocent, for how would you like to be a decedent of either Daniel Boone or Davy Crocket and be faced with the startling realization that your relative "didn't measure up?"

With having our beloved cousin Micky back in the fold, we once again proceeded to enjoy our summer together exploring and adventuring once again. As I explained earlier, we were all cousins that is except Micky and Dean, they were not cousins, but actually Micky was Dean's uncle. Micky's mother was also the mother of Dean's mother, which was kind of complicated but not really too hard to understand once you knew the family.

The Dragline

Needless to say to keep things from getting complicated, we just told everyone we were all cousins. It was a smooth way of keeping the confusion down and with us boys, the less trying to explain things the better, unless we were caught doing something we shouldn't. If that happened, then we each insisted on plenty of time to explain our sides of just what had led up to whatever we were caught doing.

Micky lived in the country with his folks, while Dean lived in the big city of Boise. Dean although a good kid to pal around with, he was a city boy and dumber than a rock when it came to the wild country life. But that summer he spent with us other boys, we taught him a great deal. He remarked for years "What I learned from them Matthews boys, served me better than all the survival training the military had to offer." Having survived that summer with us, he had later gone on to be a highly decorated army Special Forces soldier and served his country in Iraq, Afghanistan and several other mid-east adventures. But I'm getting ahead of myself.

Where Micky was of a thin rail build, he was "wang leather tough" and as with the ride and sudden stop atop the Jacks Fork, he had to be.

Dean on the other hand, was a round faced, heavy set lad and was what we referred to as "Rollie Poley". The lad liked his food, and everyone else's given the chance, but he wouldn't be left behind. Well, I guess I should say, he didn't want to be left behind, but on several occasions as we were in full retreat from danger, I'm afraid to say, like it or not, he was.

Dean being the biggest of us, was usually the last one to arrive and the one always bringing up the rear when we were fleeing for our lives. And just as luck would have it, the very next day we ran into that huge beehive down at the crick. I had spotted the clump of bees and my younger brother Ike had been goaded

Archie Matthews

into throwing that rock at it. There had been a mad dash for anywhere other than right where those bees were at. And as I and Ike had made it to the far bend in the crick, and looked back, there wasn't much question as to who was going to arrive next, hobbling Micky or Rollie Poley Dean. I will say this for Micky, even though that broken arm in a sling and the back brace surely slowed him down. He could flat pick up and lay down that big old boot of his dads, especially when there was a cloud of bees the size of the state of Oregon hot after him. But poor Dean, he was chugging along with his tongue hung out like an over taxed hound dog, sweat pouring from every pore of his body. His flailing arms and his jumping and screaming told us he wasn't quite escaping the front line of angry bees. But just as he reached us and crumpled into a heap or gasping still rippling rolls of flesh, the bees must have decided they'd punished him enough and turned and dissipated in the distance.

Boy-howdy, I remember thinking he couldn't keep up that extremely loud pitch screaming for long, as grandma kept swabbing each newfound bee sting with mercurochrome. There were so many stings on him, she'd have needed a couple of blacksmith bellows to blow all those "owies" better. I will say this, Dean looked like a chunky version of the Devil himself, that night as he got undressed for bed, all he'd needed was the pointed tail. He was red from head to toe what with all that red mercurochrome slathered on him. Not to mention his cranky disposition and the evil look he'd gained after our little adventure. It was a long night of discontent as us four boys piled upstairs and shared the big brass bed for the night. What with Micky and his pokey splints, not to mention that hard metal back brace I was constantly banging my elbow against all night long. Not to mention Dean's thrashing swollen limbs and his cranky accusing, "It's all your fault Arch, you put Ike up to it. It's all your fault"

The Dragline

Needless to say after the bee episode, we were strongly encouraged to stay close to home by grandma and her request had been sharply punctuated by her snapping that willow switch.

That's when we decided to spend some time down to grandpa's scrap yard. There were all kinds of stuff there that we could play around and explore, with little interference from adults. Grandma felt comfortable since we were just outside the back yard fence and behind the blacksmith shop. Close enough she could stroll out and check up on us, let alone easy to get to should an emergency rescue vehicle need to be called. Hence, Mr. Wellner's daughter Joyce and her siren equipped station wagon.

Needless to say grandpa wasn't very happy to have us "rapscallions" as he called us, "Marauding around in his scrap pile". Although I didn't know what "marauding" meant, I did get the impression that whatever it was, grandpa was concerned about his iron. He'd also grumbled something about us "Terrorizing the rest of the country" as he had put it. There were even a growl or two along the lines, "We had been set on his door step by ingrate children that were even now, doing their best to drive him stark raving mad, with their prodigy". Although I didn't understand those words at the time, I understood he wasn't happy and so we tried our best to stay out of his hair for a time. But you know what they say about the "Best laid plans of mice and men". All I can say is, if we'd have known what was coming, we'd have stuck to that plan and stayed out of his hair....or should I say "Dragline".

We had begun playing on and in the half dozen old vehicles that sat around the scrap yard, and then soon we had graduated into climbing up and over a couple huge caterpillars that had been

Archie Matthews

parked behind the shop and left to rust. They were huge faded yellow metal earth moving tanks that grandpa had once used many years ago in his logging and mining operations, or so dad had explained. We were all over them working this lever and that, pushing buttons and flicking switches. Dean was sitting on the huge bench seat of one machine with little Micky setting beside him. They were shouting at me and Ike as we sat on the other shouting back. We played for hours out there and had a wonderful time and then before we knew it, grandma was at the fence shouting lunch was ready.

We all ran for the house, except Micky who hobbled and Dean who waddled more than ran. We piled into the house and sat down at the dining room table and grandpa said grace after a few minutes of grandma trying to quiet us down. We quickly ate and were just about ready to charge back outside when grandpa stopped us with a look.

"You boys can play out there on those cats, you can terrorize those cars and you can mess around back there in my scrap yard, but you stay off of that dragline! I'll hide you if I catch you mess' n with it." And he gave a double dose of his stern look as emphasis.

Poor old grandpa, he hadn't a clue what "reverse psychology was", for if he had, he would have realized, he had just instructed us to "MESS WITH THE DRAGLINE !"

We had all stopped and faithfully listened and dutifully bobbed our heads in the "Yes we understand direction." But as any parent up to date on reverse psychology will attest, it didn't mean a thing. For each of us although we understood and spoke English, we were also kids and had heard precisely the opposite of what was spoken.

The Dragline

The minute we had re-entered the scrap yard, we were drawn to the side of the huge yellow and black drag line. The drag line was a enormous brute that set up on huge tracks like the caterpillars had, but it had a large body with an enclosed cab that swiveled on a huge gear atop the tracks. The cab consisted of a large steel door with a glass window that slid back and forth in a track. The front of the cab was a huge two piece automotive glass window that had a thick steel bar about waist high that separated the bottom half from the top. Inside the cab was a cracked leather seat with its horse hair stuffing poking out in several places. In front of the chair were several levers set atop a steel dash full of gauges, lights and dials. Then there on the floor directly in front of the seat were several large steel foot pedals, one of which had a large steel wrench wedged against it and the bottom of the console, firmly pressing it down to the floor. Of course the inside of the cab was viewed through the closed glass door as we stood upon the huge track and peered inside. We were just getting a good look, when the back door to the blacksmith shop swung open and grandpa stuck his head out and shouted, "Hey, you kids, get away from that dragline!"

We all jumped down and ran for the distant section of the scrap yard that held other than the dragline. Well most of us had jumped, Micky had actually tumbled off the track, but had quickly regained his feet, big boot and all, and hobbled close behind. Upon reaching the safety of the more secluded part of the scrap yard, and not within striking distance of grandpa, we all began to play without another thought about the dragline. (Yeah, right).

Although we kept back and away from the dragline for the remainder of the day, I had been sitting atop the caterpillar thinking, while the rest of the fellows had been mindlessly having fun.

Archie Matthews

I had noticed the dragline also had a huge steel boom that reached far aloft at a forty five degree angle. Of course I didn't know about angles, other than when my arm or leg got bent into an un-natural one. I had noticed that boom sported a long steel cable that originated from the back of the cab from a huge circular drum like a giant fishing reel. At this end of the cable, was a big hook and just above the big hook was a large steel ball. Both of which were pulled up to the bottom of the boom and held in place with an old twist of rope.

Since I was a bright kid with a vivid imagination, I could envision myself sitting atop that huge ball swinging from the top of the blacksmith shop to clear above and beyond the woodshed behind the house. And what a boy can think of, a boy can do, or so my motto went. All I had to do was figure out a way to distract grandpa away from the shop so we could put my plan into action.

The next day, as us four boys were at the breakfast table when grandma let slip some interesting information. Grandpa it seems had to go down to Sweet, a small town about thirty miles South down the long narrow valley. Grandma had explained, grandpa had some pieces he'd repaired to deliver to a fellow down there and was going to do some picking up of some stuff that needed repaired. The long and short of the conversation was, the dragline was about to be unguarded. This also meant, I began to feel the thrill of swinging off the top of the shop and into the wild blue yonder as I finished my toast.

After breakfast us four boys set out for the scrap yard and being the oldest and the "Ringleader" as grandma always described, or the "Instigator" as grandpa put it, I called a meeting. We immediately all huddled close and I began to lay out "The Plan", for riding the dragline cable.

Now my brother Ike wasn't what I'd consider the sharpest knife in the cupboard, but he was considered a veritable "Genius" compared to either Micky or Dean. I will say this for Ike, whether from past experiences or a natural desire towards survival, he was getting harder and harder to talk into being the first to try anything exciting. But I will give him this, he would sit and listen to my ideas, it's just his facial expressions became more and more accusing with every adventure we embarked together on.

I began by pointing out the obvious benefits of swinging around on the cable and everyone's heads were bobbing the right direction. Everyone's eyes kept darting from the dragline boom to the top of the blacksmith shop. And just as everyone was deep into imagining just what fun riding the end of that cable was going to be like, I saw Ike's eyes slowly swing to me and he squinted an accusing look and said, "Who's going to be the first one to give that a try?"

"Hmmm...." I stalled, as I slowly looked from Ike to Micky and then at Dean.

"Who wants to go first?" I asked as innocently as I could, not particularly wanting to try it first myself. My many past experiences had often taught me, if something was going to go wrong, it usually took out the first guy to give it a try. I was partial to not being taken out, I and Ike were brothers after all, and I too had some of that Survival instinct in me.

Dean perked right up and his arm shot into the air, "Me Arch, pick me!" That's when I knew I had my guinea pig and we were good to go.

"Well, I should be the first one to go, since I'm the oldest, but come to think of it, you hardly ever get to go first." I replied a bit reluctantly, not wanting to reel this big fish in to quickly and risk losing him. "I suppose it's about time you get to be the first one to have a good time and the rest of us can just wait our turns."

Archie Matthews

I'd have whacked Ike aside the head for the disgusted knowing look he was giving me, but I didn't want to startle the rest of the herd. Therefore I just quickly dodged the look and we jumped right into the planning stage.

The way I saw it, we were going to need a long rope to tie onto the hook and pull it to the roof of the shop. Since the top of the dragline was just a few feet shy of the roof, and there were ladder rungs running right up the side of the cab, accessing the roof was going to be a piece of cake. All we needed was to somehow pull that hook and ball up to the roof, and I planned on doing that with a long rope.

We all set about looking for a long piece of rope, but you'd be amazed just how scarce a rope can be in a metal scrap yard. We searched everywhere, including inside the woodshed and on both the front and back porch. We'd just about looked everywhere when grandma caught on we were looking for something and stepped outside.

"Ike, what are all you boys looking around for?" she asked a bit suspiciously.

I heard her from around the corner where I had frozen listening intently. My heart almost sank and I imagined hearing a can opening and the beans about to be spilled. But I have to give it to Ike, he'd evidently learned a thing or two in his years of being my brother, for he never missed a beat when he said, "Well, Arch lost his sling shot and we wanted to go to the crick and shoot squirrels, so we're look' n where he might have lost it."

I imagine that's the kind of smooth talk old P.T Barnum had used to "smooze" people into the circus with, it was smooth, mighty smooth and grandma just nodded and off she went, not a word wiser.

138

The Dragline

I came around the corner and gave Ike a smile and nod and then gathered up Micky and Dean for another huddle session out by the woodshed.

"I got an idea." I began, when Dean interrupted me. "Say Arch, I know where there's a long stretch of rope."

"Where?" Micky quickly asked.

"Up to Ace's barn, the Jackson Fork rope", Dean explained with a huge smile.

"Oh, that rope." Micky said, as his poor battered body gave a bit of a quiver at the very mention of the "Fork of Doom", as Micky called it for years after his ordeal.

"I was just going to say that very thing!" I exclaimed quickly.

I instantly got another of those scalding looks from my dear sweet younger brother, but I just ignored it. "Micky you better stay here and the rest of us will go." I added.

"That way, if grandma asks where we are you can tell her we went to the crick, and you didn't want to get your boot all wet' n muddy. The rest of us will go and get the rope and be back soon." I explained.

Leaving Micky behind the three of us were off to Ace's barn. I'd left Micky behind not to answer any questions from grandma, for I knew as long as we weren't making a ruckus, she wasn't going to worry. I'd wanted Micky to stay behind because of that hobbling boot. He and his boot wouldn't do us any good where we were headed. We needed quick feet and unbroken bones where we were going. Ace's barn was amid a big pasture with several huge bulls that needed distracting by someone that could run fast. By distracting the bulls in one direction, the other two could race to the barn and pilfer the rope and escape before they

Archie Matthews

got trampled or gored. Now all I had to do was convince Ike that he was the fleetest of foot and somehow get him to lead off the bulls.

Ike being my younger brother had been born with an inordinate amount of caution. Dad often mentioned, where I didn't have much restraint in tempting fate, Ike had gotten enough for both of us. Keeping this in mind, I knew I was going to have to approach this one with caution, I decided to wait until the last minute to broach the subject with him, and then, suddenly we were at Ace's pasture fence and the decision had to be made.

"I'll run the bulls, and you and Dean make for the barn and get the rope." Ike immediately offered.

Talk about throw a stick in the spokes of my mental wheel, suddenly I stopped in my tracks and gave Ike a cautious look.

"Wha.....?" I started to stammer.

"I'll run the bulls. Deans to slow and would be instant mush under the bulls hoof. I'm no good at untangling ropes, so you're going to have to do that." Ike explained, realizing I had it all planned, but his volunteering to take the bulls on had taken me completely by surprise.

"Okay, sounds good." Was all I could stammer without spending most of the afternoon figuring out the real reason he had volunteered to take on the most dangerous part of the whole plan. And with that, Ike shot over the stile and was off like a shot.

In our part of Idaho the ground was covered with rocks. Most people couldn't and didn't even try, to drive post holes in the ground, instead they constructed rock cribs to hold up their fencing wire. Ace's pasture was no different and therefore, about every fifty feet or so was a wooden slatted box filled full of rocks called "rock cribs". In between the rock cribs, about every ten feet or so was a wooden slat nailed to the wire just sitting upon the top of the ground. These slats didn't really do anything other than keep the wire properly spaced and giving the appearance the fence was solid.

Now since trying to crawl through barb wire stretched tight on the wobbly slats was so hard to part and make ones way through, we also had "Stiles". A stile was a set of steps that went up and over the wire and down the other side, allowing humans to go up and over, yet keeping the horses and cows inside. Most pastures had a stile, and it was at this point in the fence that Ike had crossed over the fence and headed across the pasture waving his hat and yelling for all he was worth.

This particular field also lay on the quickest route to the local favorite fishing and swimming hole, we were well versed in crossing the bull occupied pasture. Usually it wasn't much of an obstacle, but this time of year, early summer, it still held the majority of Ace's bulls and the danger increased considerably with ever bull. If I'd have taken a guess, I'd have said there were around six or seven in that six acre pasture. That worked out to a lot of bull for one kid to distract and hope to come out the other side, alive.

Ike had gone over the stile like a rocket and was running along and shouting, while waving his hat and immediately the bulls had raised their heads from grazing and had taken up the challenge of running down the skinny interloper. Seeing the bulls fall right in behind Ike, I and Dean also shot over the stile and headed at an angle for the barn in the opposite direction Ike was headed, more or less. We were almost to barn when Ace's big cream colored bull, "Hitler" came charging around the corner to see what all the shouting was about.

Archie Matthews

I never did know who had named that bull or why it was called "Hitler", I just know that's what everyone called him. Little did I know it was because Hitler, as his German namesake, wanted to exterminate anybody not German, and since all of us had been born Americans, we figured we were definitely on his hit list. Hitler had always acted like the only good American kid was a trampled American kid.

In seeing Hitler round the corner of the barn, I and Dean shifted gears and went into "Over-drive". Or at least I should say, I did, it seems Dean was already in his highest gear, and if anything, due to the long distance we'd already run, he had to shift down a notch just to keep going. This presented a slow moving target for Hitler, and one of which even as a dumb brute, he was immediately ready to cash in on. Therefore seeing me pick up speed, Hitler lowered his head and set his sights for the "huffing and puffing" staggering larger target bringing up the rear.

I had made the barn and quickly opened one side of the big double doors and turned to see Dean was not going to make it without a horn in his backside. Since Dean was kin, I knew I couldn't just stand by and let him get a horn in the butt. Thinking fast, I dashed by Dean, and started throwing rocks at Hitler.

Everyone that knew me as a kid will tell you, "Arch is a heck of a rock chucker". I not only could send quantities down range almost fast enough to rival modern machine guns, but I was a mighty good shot. One rock after the other began to ricochet off Hitler's fast approaching lowered head. And then one particularly lucky shot beaned him right smack dab in the eye.

If you've ever seen a semi slam on the brakes while pulling a massive trailer, you can imagine what happened as Hitler's front hooves immediately stopped, yet his rear end was still going. Instantly the back of that bull whipped around and "Jack Knifed". In one huge cloud of dust, over he went and rolled about three times before he got to his feet. Hitler having rolled over and raising a cloud of dust the size of the barn itself, gained his feet and just stood there. Seeing Hitler go down, just as Dean passed by me, I whirled and fell right in behind him and in two seconds we were in the barn shutting the doors behind us.

Being boys, weren't long on congratulating one another on survival, at our age, we defied death a dozen times a day, and with that said, we climbed into the loft. I'd like to say we made short work of untangling the rope from the elaborate pulley system, but it took longer than I'd imagined. But once we realized it was actually three ropes through three different sets of pulleys, we got the upper hand and sorted it out quick. To get enough slack to get the rope free, we had to push the Jackson Fork to the very edge of the loft doors and prop it up precariously against the one side. Leaving it precariously balanced, I made a quick mental note, not to walk beneath it on our way out. A stiff wind and that Jackson Fork would come crashing down, but being a kid, I didn't give that much thought. A few minutes later we had a huge coil of rope and were peeking out the side door, trying to decide if it was safe enough to make a mad dash back to the stile or not.

We could see Hitler, although still a bit dazed, head down by the big double doors just waiting for a couple of foolish kids to poke their heads out, so he could trample us into good American's. Assured that if we slid out the side door and moved straight for the stile, Hitler wouldn't be able to see us until the last minute. Then Dean went to the back door and announced Ike was at the far end of the pasture still holding their attention.

With everything lined up in our favor to the best of our ability, I gathered up the coil of rope and threw it over my head and one arm, and gave Dean a nod and we bolted out the door. Nothing on earth can make a kid run like the fear of death. My dad was fond of saying, "The fear of punishment was greater than the hope of reward." And he'd raised us boys with the thorough understanding of that little proverb. Although I was hoping to make it back to the dragline and have fun, it wasn't near as big a motivator in this instance as the fear of getting gored and trampled, therefore, I hauled ass…..and rope.

We were a bit more than half way when tubby cousin Dean actually passed me. Just the fact that Dean passed me, told me I was severely slowed down by that pile of rope. But the other thing it told me was a bull was hot on our trail and Dean had seen him and been spurred to greater speed. Worse yet, as he went by, he yelled something at me, but since my heart was already pounding in my ears, I hadn't heard his words, but I imagined they were words of impending doom. Although terror was welling up in me, my body was doing its best to go as fast as it could to survive. My mind began screaming for my body to off load the rope ASAP or else.

Usually a boy my age doesn't heed his brain as much as he should; mostly we follow what our body tells us. Our stomachs say its hungry, we eat. Our body says it's thirsty, we drink. Our bodies say, time to water the mule, we water. At the age of ten, about the only thing my mind was much good for, was figuring out how to get my body in or out of trouble. After all, that's why my parents insisted I go to school, so that I would develop my mind, which at the time, I thought was an enormously wasted amount of time. But in this instance my mind was trying to make sure the body survived and therefore, my body began to listen intently.

I began to struggle with divesting myself of the multiple rope coils hanging around my head and shoulders banging against my hip with every step. I tried to grab the coils and heave them over my head and down my arm and free myself, but in my haste, I didn't

The Dragline

get but about half the coils. As I threw the first half of the coils off, and then tried to reach up and finish the task with the remaining coils around my head calamity stuck. The result of ridding myself of only half the coils of rope presented an instant problem as the section of rope I'd shed caught the ground and pulled tight the remaining coils. Worse yet, there had been one coil between the two bundles that had looped around my neck. One minute I was running for my life, the next moment I instantly became the outlaw at the end of a short rope, and suddenly I hit the end.

I remember my feet shooting up to the height of my head and seeing one shoe keep going, and hitting Dean right on the forehead as he for some reason stopped at the stile and stood there looking at me with a smile on his face. I also remember catching the glint of my silver belt buckle in the sun, at that split second my body was straight out before me, hanging in midair for the briefest of seconds, before the lights went out in Georgia, or should I say in Idaho.

Thank God for small miracles, like being unconscious when one is hung on his feet at a dead run and slammed on his back. Although I remember everything appearing to happen in slow motion, I think it all happened so fast, I had hit my head on the ground before the pain had caught up to me.

I couldn't have been out for more than a second or two, for when I opened my eyes, Dean was just waddling over to me, he was slow but not that slow, so I was sure it was but a second or two. I remember trying to take a big breath because my lungs were screaming for air, but mouth agape and work my jaws as I did, no air was coming in. Then Dean bent down and pulled the trailing rope enough to give me some slack around the deadly coil about my neck, and the air whistled in.

Archie Matthews

I rolled over and not seeing instant death upon us, I looked at Dean and asked, "What were you shouting about as you passed me? I thought Hitler was hot on our trail?"

He just looked down at me and innocently said, "I said, I'd beat you to the stile". The sudden realization, that's what he had shouted as he'd passed me. If I'd had more time, and didn't hurt so much, I'd have jumped up and boxed the idiot's ears for sending me into a panic the way he had. But in looking around, I could see Ike trotting around the far corner of the pasture making his way around the outside fence. Close behind was the herd of agitated bulls still seeking a way to get some trampling in on their quarry.

It took but a few moments to coil the rope back up and donning it once again around my head and shoulders, I was up and over the stile with Dean close behind. A few minutes later Ike showed up and right behind him but on the opposite side of the fence was his horned fan club bellowing their disappointment as we left them behind, without a single kid trampled.

Easing back through town and up the road beside the house, we ducked behind the woodshed. As we had approached the woodshed we noticed grandpa's truck was gone and knew we were free to begin having fun. Keeping the woodshed between us and the house, just in case grandma happened to be in the back yard, we picked up Micky as we went by, then made a dash for the scrap yard. We slowly picked our way to the dragline and set about making our preparations.

I tied a big loop in the one end of the rope and then climbed up on the dragline track and up the boom until I got to where the hook lay pulled up against the boom and tied with a short piece of half rotted rope. After getting our long rope in place, I used my old Barlow pocket knife to cut through the rotted rope holding the boom and set free, the hook and ball with long cable

The Dragline

attached swung free and far over the scrap yard. Then I sent Ike, Dean and Micky around to the front of the blacksmith shop and told them to wait there for me. I then grabbed the other end of the rope and up the ladder rungs set into the cab of the dragline, up to its very top and crept along the back to the edge that ended just a couple feet from the shop roof. I coiled up the rope and threw it across to the very low pitched steel roof of the blacksmith shop. Then with a short running leap, I jumped the gap and landed with a clattering bang beside the rope coils. It was a matter of seconds and I was up and over the roof to the front edge of the shop and dropped the rope down to my awaiting conspirators.

"Now you guys pull the rope until I can get ahold of the hook, then find something to tie it to." I instructed them quickly.

The three of them began to back up and soon had the hook and ball with cable attached within grasp at the roofs edge.

"There you go!" I had shouted, "Now tie it off somewhere!" I instructed as I took ahold of the hook and ball and knew we could release the rope from the hook at launch time. A few minutes later back around the shop came the boys and Dean began insisting he had been the one to go first. Ike was eyeballing the whole contraption with his critical eye for survival and therefore he wasn't arguing about who was going first, unless someone suggested it be him. Micky was sitting on the edge of the dragline track still catching his breath from the long arduous hobble around the blacksmith shop and back again. He wasn't going to argue the point about Dean going first either, so that left me and Dean.

Now by rights, I had been the one to think the whole exciting ride on the dragline cable up and although I had some doubts about it at first, upon seeing my idea come to fruition, I was now entertaining second thoughts about who should go first. I and

Dean haggled a few minutes and I did everything I could to convince him I should go first, but Dean was pretty adamant that he'd been "Promised" and wasn't going to be cheated out of it. Therefore I finally relented and I and Dean climbed up the ladder to the top of the dragline and crossed to the roof and Dean scrambled up the hook and sat atop the big steel ball with the cable between his legs.

"Hold on tight Dean, you let go and you'll go splat and that'll be the end of you." I warned. I struggled with slipping the rope up the hook and freeing it, but after several minutes of inching it along, it suddenly slipped loose and Dean shot out into the open air.

What a wonderful swing that was, for the heavy ball carried that cable way out and over the scrap yard and then for a split second from my vantage point my breath caught as I saw Dean fast approaching the side of the woodshed. From my vantage point it looked like Dean's swing was going to end abruptly at the end of the woodshed and I held my breath for a brief second and tensed up waiting for the "Splat" and subsequent "Scream" of pain as Dean collided. But then the ball with tubby kid attached cleared the wood shed roof and slowing, reached its appendix and then reversed course and came swinging back. As the whole apparatus with tightly clutched kid returned I heard myself and my brother and cousin Micky all shouting encouragement for the swing was magnificent.

As Dean approached and the cable, ball and hook slowed down, I quickly reached out with the rope and dropped the loop over the hook. Unfortunately as the whole swinging contraption came to a sudden stop, Dean lost his grip and came crashing to the roof top at my very feet, all but sliding off the edge of the roof, onto a large pile of jagged steel beneath. But as he hit the roof, I

The Dragline

reached down and grabbed the back of his pants and held him at the brink and then slowly helped him get to his feet.

In noticing the look on Dean's face, I wasn't quite sure what to make of it, whether it was terror from swinging or terror of realizing he'd almost slid off the roof onto a pile of jagged steel.

"Well?" I asked Dean, "What did you think?"

Dean stuttered a second and said, "Dern if I know, it felt scary, but I had my eyes closed the whole time."

Everyone broke out laughing and then even Dean began laughing. "I'm next!" I shouted and clambered aboard the large steel ball and grabbed the steel cable. "Work the rope loose Dean, and be ready to slip the loop back over the hook when I swing back."

Dean struggled and struggled with the rope to get it loose but to no avail and seeing we needed another hand, Ike quickly scrambled to the roof and as Dean pulled the cable back, Ike got enough slack to slip the rope and away I went.

I'd like to tell you I shouted with glee as I swung far above all that jagged steel below. I'd also like to tell you that as I approached the wood shed, I was shouting and enjoying the exhilarating ride, but that would be far from the truth as to how that first swing felt. Until I had swung far aloft and looked out wide eyed just how high up I was actually swinging above that jagged scrap pile, I hadn't thought about the height aspect. And then I slowly spun around on the cable and was soaring backwards and saw the boys all jumping and shouting and I received a slight rush of euphoria. And then slowly spinning back around, I was just in time to view the upper end of the woodshed roof rapidly approaching and immediately felt like a fly with a rapidly approaching fly swatter must feel. I screwed my eyes tight shut

Archie Matthews

and tensed up waiting for the impact, but then felt the woodshed rush by just under my dangling feet and I took a quick peek out one eye and realized I was safe and sound.

Upon realizing I had cleared the woodshed roof like Dean had done on his turn, and reaching the end of the pendulous swing, began to slow and for that briefest half second, stopped midair and I could see clear over the shop and had a magnificent view of the gas station/café. I began shouting with glee as the backswing carried me back to the blacksmith shop roof and upon coming over the roof, I slipped off the ball and dropped to my feet as Dean and Ike slipped the noose over the hook and stopped the ball for the next rider.

I won't bore you by describing our ride after ride out into the wild blue yonder, each taking turns and each of us getting bolder and bolder with our shouting and leg swinging far above the earth. We had each taken several trips up and over and back and we were hooting and hollering and having a fantastic time and all but forgot about the time of day. And in that lack of discretion we soon met our doom. For Dean was just leaving the roof top on his way towards the woodshed, when standing up from releasing the hook, I saw grandpa's truck in front of the shop and suddenly heard the back door of the shop open with a "BANG".

Although the banging of the door was just that, a door flying open, it might as well have been the starting pistol to a worldwide running event. For as the door banged open and grandpa leapt out screaming, kids shot in every direction. Ike having been sitting on the edge of the dragline track, jumped up and dodged into the open cab door and banged it shut behind him. Micky had been coming back from "watering his mule "in the outhouse between the scrap yard and the house. Suddenly seeing grandpa appear through the "Banging" door, Micky hobbled on

150

The Dragline

up the trail for the house, doing his best impression of a cross country track star, with one exception, that big hobbling boot.

Since I was standing right above grandpa's head on the roof, and had no place to hide, I instinctively ran over the roof top and hunkered down just on the other side of the peak. In peering over the top of the roof, I saw tragedy unfold as quickly as grandfather had predicted. Dean having reached the end of his swing over the woodshed hung for the milli-second midair and I saw his head swivel with a huge smile hanging just briefly. And then suddenly I saw the boom of the dragline as if in slow motion, go crashing down to the ground stretching far across the scrap yard. As if time had stopped, I saw Dean's face change from the height of wondrous exhilaration, to the crashing depths of doom.

Time is a strange thing, for many times upon just such a tragic occurrence I've had the misfortune of seeing time slow down to where even the minutest details could be observed, in gory detail. This time was no different and I noticed not only the realization upon Deans face that he was crashing to earth, but I noticed the ever increasing wet spot soaking through his trousers. My eyes swiveled down to look through the window of the dragline cab and saw Ike crouched down on the floorboard amidst the steel foot pedals, and suddenly realized that must have been what that wedged wrench was doing, "Holding up the boom", by depressing that pedal. I saw the startling realization upon Ike's face as he realized he had just accidently sent poor pudgy Dean to his death.

In that seemingly endless drag of time, my eyes also took in grandpa in mid jump and between shouts, and I heard his long slow drag of air as he inhaled preparing for another. I also saw poor little hobbling Micky, as the shadow of the boom slowly began to descend upon him as his every muscle strained to force his already patched and brace covered body out from underneath the impeding squash.

I'll also never forget in the briefest of instances, seeing grandma coming out of the back porch, with dish rag in hand, and the wide eyed horror across her face as she took everything in as I have just described.

I often think back and wonder if time nearly stopping actually ran in the family, because I could have sworn, I saw her eyes swiveling just as rapidly as mine, and the horror on her face rapidly switching channels as mine had. First to the channel viewing the helplessness of Dean on his trajectory of doom; Micky and his bandaged body struggling to avoid being snuffed out by the avalanche of collapsing steel; Ike's terror filled eyes peeking over the dragline dashboard taking in the result of his knocking the wrench loose setting everything into motion; and then my own frozen immobility there amid the roof top of the shop, my eyes darting and swiveling ten times the speed of sound.

And then as it always does, time rushed forward in the blink of an eye and caught up with everything that came crashing down.

A deafening crash of groaning twisted steel and squashed scrap steel and smashed car bodies filled the air, as did a mountain of dust suddenly obscuring everyone's vision of the carnage and broken bodies beneath. And then as if someone had hit the mute button on the television remote control, there was a sudden silence.

The briefest of seconds ticked by and then bedlam ensued once again. Grandpa having filled his lungs, began to speak in the proverbial "Tongues" the preacher had once talked about. You know where a person of biblical background begins to shout words that no one can understand, even the person speaking them.

Grandma ran through the back gate, and when I say "through the gate", I mean right through the gate, without even stopping to open it. She reached little Micky's side as he stood as anchored to the one spot. His body stock still and not even trembling, the only movement being his face was twitching and blinking and his mouth kept opening and closing without uttering a sound. Not to worry though, he soon found his voice, but even through adulthood, his face would twitch and blink uncontrollably whenever he came under stressful situations. I seem to remember they called it some kind of "psychosis" or something. But suddenly upon realizing grandma was there at his side and just inches away lay the enormous boom of the dragline, barely missing him by a hairs breadth. That's when little Micky found his screaming mechanism and fired it up and cranked the volume to high.

Ike slowly stood up and slid the cab door back on its track and stepped out, looking from me to grandpa, then on to grandma and Micky. Suddenly grandpa began speaking English again and with a shout, charged up the boom towards where the long cable crossed over the top of both the caterpillars and off into the tangle of vegetation surrounding the small crick that ran along behind the woodshed.

"Dean....Dean....." grandpa shouted as he dodged this pile and that following the cable to its gristly end.

I slowly sat down on the roof peak and brought my knees to my chest, and sat my chin sadly down atop. Knowing the chances of poor chubby cousin Dean surviving that sling shot at the end of the dragline cable was about as slim as that robin egg I had tried to shoot out of my sling shot last summer. It hadn't ended well for the egg and I strongly suspected the "smooshed" results

Archie Matthews

were going to be about the same with Dean. The egg hadn't even successfully exited the sling shot but had instantly turned to mush while still in the leather pocket. "The force of the pressure and acceleration meeting the drag coefficient had just been too much." Or so my grandfather had explained seeing the result of my failed experiment and laughing mightily at the time.

Suddenly I heard a shout from the far off tangle of vegetation surround the crick and back up the trail came grandpa carrying a huge muddy bundle.

"He's alive, he's alive", he kept shouting, which immediately reminded me of the television program "Frankenstein" where the mad scientist Dr. Frankenstein bringing his horrid creation of sewn together human parts alive, begins yelling the same thing.

But in Grandpa's case, he carried a huge bulk of oozing mud, with an exposed ear and half recognizable human hand protruding as well as a foot with a stark white sock still attached. Grandpa shot up the trail along the collapsed boom and through the demolished gate grandma had gone through. He quickly lay his mud covered bundle on the grass by the back porch door and grabbed a hose and began soaking through the mud trying to find the remaining human parts beneath.

Upon hearing Dean wasn't dead and was still clinging to life, I quickly climbed off the roof top and joining Ike by the dragline we both quickly caught up to grandma and the hobbling Micky as we all made our way to grandpa and Dean.

Grandpa was making vast progress in clearing huge amounts of mud from Dean's arms and legs as well as around his face and as we all stepped close behind grandpa, we saw Dean's eyes flutter and open.

I have to give it to Dean, he wasn't a cry baby by any means and he startled all of us by slowly smiling. "Well hello grandpa, did you have a nice trip?" You could have heard a pin drop at that moment in time for the only sound was a slow in rush of air as grandpa began to take a huge breath and said, "Dern you kids…..you're going to be the death of me yet."

Dean just blinked and continued to smile and said, "Not today grandpa, I think we both survived today. But I don't know about tomorrow."

We needn't go into details about the heartwarming hugs all around at the realization we'd all just escaped death and amazingly enough, even dismemberment. I also don't feel the need to mention the short lived celebration quickly took a turn towards a "Punishment Phase" that lasted way longer then the healing of all the strains, sprains and bruises. Although some of those were directly attributed to the Punishment Phase.

It seems the only long lasting casualty of the whole "Dragline Fiasco" as it is still referred to in my family, was the dragline itself. Since the boom was in pieces and a tangle of jumbled bent steel, the dragline was doomed to become true scrap and over the years, slowly disappeared a piece at a time.

Days later while we kids were playing behind the blacksmith shop, I had the good fortune to hear Ace bemoaning to grandpa about his bull Hitler. It seemed somehow the Jacks fork had somehow become dislodged at the edge of the hay loft far above and sometime during the night had come crashing down. Ace was adamant there should have been a third rope keeping the Jacks fork from crashing down, but for the life of him he couldn't figure out what happened to it. But it seems without that third rope, the Jacks fork had crashed to the ground, yet not quite to the ground, for Hitler had been caught between the jacks' fork and the ground. Ace said he was offering cut and wrapped hamburger to anyone and everyone for fifty cents a pound. Which evidently from the startled look on grandpa's face, I took to mean was a very good price.

For upon hearing that he slowly looked over to the corner where he had us coil that old rope and stored it in his shop, and then with a slow deliberate swivel of his head, he looked right into my eye, as it was pressed up to and looking through my favorite knothole through the back wall.

It's a funny thing how some members of a close knit family such as ours can communicate via just a look. For right then and there, I distinctly heard grandpa loud and clear, thinking…… "Don't you ever mention that rope or where it came from." Yup, loud and clear.

The Dragline

The Hair Raising "Yowl"

In my fifty plus years in this world, I've heard a lot of hair raising things in my lifetime. I've heard car crashes and screams; I've watched horror shows with actors and actresses screaming on both television and the big screen. I've watched kids terrified and howling at every kind of hair raising event. But when I was seven years old I heard a hair raising "Yowl" one dark summer night that still brings a chill to my spine just thinking about it.

Like years before, I was out of school and spending the summer with my grandparents in the sleepy little town of Ola, Idaho or I should say, it was sleepy until the "Yowl". I can assure you as a lad of seven and scared to death of the dark, there wasn't much sleeping before the "Yowl", unless it was snuggled up tight to a night light. Yet after the "Yowl" started, nights were long drawn out affairs full of wide eyed, sweat filled hours, imagining all kinds of horrors lurking about. Furthermore, I must admit, when the "hair raising Yowl" began, even during the full light of day, I was one edgy customer.

It all started one summer's eve as my grandparents and I sat out on the front porch after dinner. Grandma was sitting in her rocking chair knitting as usual with her ugly little dog Festus by her side. Grandpa was sitting in his chair sharpening his pocket knife on a large gray whetstone. I was sitting on the wide wooden bannister that surrounded the porch fiddling with my cap gun, when a far off "Yowl" of something in dire pain and/or lingering death sounded.

For an instant all motion on the front porch ceased, except for my hair, which had instantly sprang straight up and my eyeballs, which immediately swiveled from my cap gun to first grandma and then to grandpa.

"My word!" grandma exclaimed. "What on earth was that?" she said looking up from her knitting, her own eyes swiveling about.

"I'm not sure what that was..." Grandpa replied with raised eyebrow. "It sounded like some kind of feline, bobcat maybe. But I never heard one "Yowl" like that." He remarked, his own pocket knife and whetstone frozen in his hand as his eyes swiveled first from one side of the horizon to the other.

 I even noticed grandma's dog Festus lying beside her chair, his head up and ears erect, but strangely unusual for the little bark fiend, he wasn't barking. He just lay there with his eyes big and his ears standing straight up listening intently. Any other time, the slightest strange sound would have set him to barking his head off and running around looking for whatever it was had interrupted our evening, but not tonight and not at the "Yowl".

After a few tense moments of remaining still and listening intently, everyone seemed to relax and resume their activities. Grandma went back to her "knit one pearl two", and grandpa once again began stroking his pocket knife back and forth over his course whetstone. Festus eased his ears back down and once again lay his head down upon his paws, his beady little eyes slowly swiveling around keeping close watch on all of us. I, just so happened to be the very last to let down my guard and

The Hair Raising "Yowl"

was slowly letting my raised hair settle back down into its sedative state, when once again a mournful "Yowl" broke the serene evening.

Once again everyone looked up from what they were doing, eyes swiveling this way and that, tensions once drawing taunt as a banjo string. There was an instance of absolute silence as if everyone was holding their breath waiting for someone else to say something, when Festus let out an unsuspected "howl" and jumped to his feet barking. Everyone gave such a start that pandemonium was instantly set loose on the little porch.

Grandpa had been severely startled and nearly cut his finger off. He sat there pinching his thumb where he had nicked it with his pocket knife.
"Festus!" he shouted, "Dern your hide, you almost made me amputate my thumb! You little rascal!" he growled.

"Heavens to Betsy!" grandma wailed as her backside came clear off her chair a good foot and then just as quickly re-entered the chairs springy cushion. Dropping her knitting bundle in her lap she gave Festus a harsh look and began ordering him to "Shush!", then seeing grandpa with a bleeding finger, she asked, "Are you cut bad?"

"It's just a nick, I'll be fine." Grandpa said as he sucked his thumb a second and talking it out of his mouth he affirmed it was just a small cut.

I on the other hand had dropped my cap gun and was now clutching the post that held the banister post with both hands, hearing that second "Yowl" had almost made me fall off my banister perch into the prickly evergreen bush below. I'd fallen in those sharp little bushes before, and it was nothing to look forward to. Hence my two arms wrapped tightly around that post, my eyes wide and my hair once again standing straight up, every follicle competing for the highest vantage point to get a good look at whatever terror was about to descend upon us. Those are the physical traits of a boy scared to death of the dark, his

Archie Matthews

appendages are not only always on guard for impending doom, but coiled like a spring, ready to uncoil at a moment's notice and make a run for safety.

"Was that a cougar?" I asked quickly, my saucer sized eyes swiveling back and forth from grandma to grandpa, searching for the first sign from either of them, that I should try and save myself and run inside the house.

I'd heard a cougar call described as "Hair Raising" and sounding like a woman screaming. And if that "Yowl" was anything, it was "hair raising". Although I'd never heard a woman sound like that, but of course I was just a kid then, and hadn't yet experienced the screaming of my first wife.

Being much older now and having experienced both cougar scream and the blood thirsty vocals of my first wife, I'd have to admit, they are extremely close.....extremely. (But as the saying goes, that's another story.)

"Naw," grandpa scoffed, "Not a cougar, I've heard a few of them in my time, but that wasn't it. More like a bobcat with his tail caught in a trap. Whatever it was, it sure sounded mournful. Never heard anything quite like it."

We sat there for a bit longer, ever one of us, including the little dog Festus, ears cocked half expecting another "Yowl", but it never came. After several minutes and just as my hair had begun lying back down instead of sticking straight up, I heard another and even more dreadful sound.

"You better get ready for bed and go water your mule" grandma instructed without even looking up from her knitting. I imagine even old Adolf Hitler when ordering mass human destruction, would have at least looked up from his knitting when giving such a heinous order. But not my dear sweet grandma, she just kept right on fashioning whatever it was she was knitting, oblivious that she'd just ordered me to march off to certain death and

The Hair Raising "Yowl"

destruction in the same general direction the "Yowl" had come from…..any and everywhere but right here on the porch.

One thing you must immediately come to understand, there were "NO MULES".
Yup, even though we had no livestock what so ever, let alone "Mules", ever night I was sent off to "water my mule". That's what grandma so eloquently called "going to the outhouse to take a pee". Only she insisted a fellow went to "water his mule", instead of calling it what it actually was. Grandma explained that a man "watered his mule", and then in the same token, she also insisted, "women visited the water closet." It was enormously confusing to me as a kid and after trying my best to understand the difference and failing enormously, I had just settled into watering a mule that I didn't even have.

To this very day, when I announce I am headed outside to water my mule, I get all kinds of weird looks from friends and family. My wife and daughters have tried for years to explain that I needn't announce my mule watering intentions and should just slip off outside, but I don't want any misunderstandings as to what or where I am going or doing. Therefore, I continue to announce my intentions as I go to wander my six acre "Big Montana Cattle Ranch" located in the middle of Washington State, so that there is no confusion, mules or no mules.

Upon hearing grandma suggest that I go take care of my imaginary Mules, in the very face of a "Yowling" demon, I did almost fall off backwards and into the evergreens. For even though it wasn't quite dark yet, it was close enough for me, and evidently it was close enough for the blood thirsty demon that was doing the "Yowling".

Scared as I was of the dark and the monsters that inhabited it, even twilight was a time to be wary. Not to mention we'd just heard that hair raising "Yowl" and from the same general direction the outhouse lay in, which is to say, other than here safely on the front porch. I'd rather suffer a full bladder explosion

Archie Matthews

and instant death than to be mauled and slowly devoured by whatever terror had uttered the "hair raising Yowl".

There wasn't a mirror handy, so I couldn't see the look on my own face, but dear old grandpa must have and recognized the look of terror for what it was, because he smiled and said, "Come on, I gotta go water my mule too." So we were off towards the outhouse, me and grandpa with Festus close to our heels, which was strange because the little dog usually went out behind the Woodshed by himself which, wasn't even in the same direction. Little Festus must have felt like I did, that survival was likeliest if us males stuck together, so we did.

We went out the side gate and down the path to the outhouse, I followed grandpa and Festus was close behind me. I had nonchalant'ly dropped in behind grandpa, under the guise of letting my elder go first. But what my cowardly fear induced mind was truly calculating was if that "Yowl" happened to belong to a flesh eating monster that ambushed us, grandpa being the first in line would keep it busy while I ran for help.

All I can say is this, for Festus's sake, he's darn lucky nothing did jump out at us, for if it had as close to my heels as he was, I'd have trampled him to death running for help before he'd even had a chance of getting out of the way.

As we got to the outhouse grandpa stepped aside the little trail and smiled. "You go ahead in and I'll wait here till you're done." For a split second I was all but overwhelmed with gratitude as I realized "Good ole' grandpa" was going to stand guard, but it was incredibly short lived as I suddenly realized whatever had "Yowled" might just be in the outhouse waiting for me.

Instantly ever hair on my body jumped erect and my hand began to quiver as I slowly reached out to open the outhouse door. Evidently my taking twenty minutes to open an outhouse door didn't appeal to grandpa and with a snort; he reached out and flung the door wide.

The Hair Raising "Yowl"

"See…nothing in there", he declared giving me his disgusted "There's nothing to fear look."

"Oh", how I knew that look well, for I'd seen it often enough. At least a dozen times a week I'd get startled by a bump in the night or some spooky sound once darkness had fallen and I'd bolt for an adult's side. This would usually result in one or both grandparents doing their best to convince me there was nothing to fear. Despite their reasoning, I knew better, every kid does, it's just natural grown up's, do their best to try and convince us there are no monsters. Yet, children instinctively know that with darkness we young tender morsels are surrounded by salivating meat eating ghouls that stalk us from the shadows. Furthermore, every kid also instinctively knows only light keeps monsters from throwing themselves on us and eradicating mankind in one huge gluttonous feast.

I watched TV and knew all about monsters as well as attended church and heard the pastor remark about demons. And despite how my parents and my grandparents scoffed about monsters and demons, I didn't figure our pastor would lie, let alone television.

Besides, when you're a kid and terrified to death of being slowly devoured by monsters, every little sound becomes a warning siren that a horrible death is just seconds away. Therefore I was mighty big on heeding warning signs, especially when it came to avoiding being dismembered and devoured. Hence, my opinion, a "Yowl" like the one we had heard that evening, was definitely a warning, not to be ignored. The "Yowl" hadn't been a non-descriptive sound, like a bump or a creak or indistinctive sound; it had described its originator quite vividly to my young imagination. That "Yowl" had painted a ghastly picture in the deep recesses of my mind of just what kind of monster it belonged too. But Boy Howdy, I tell you what, although it wasn't a pretty picture, even in my wildest imaginations, my fevered young brain wasn't prepared for what it actually turned out to be.

With the immediate realization there wasn't any monster awaiting me in the outhouse, I quickly stepped in and "watered my mule" as fast as ever a mule has been watered. In fact, if someone had been holding a stop watch and timed me, I'm confident I'd have placed at the top fastest time ever for watering mules. I was fast, so fast, that I was still fastening up my trousers when I turned and exited the outhouse in a hurry.

Grandpa once again gave me his disgusted look and sadly shook his head as I almost knocked him down charging back out of the outhouse. Then he stepped inside and closed the door and I was immediately faced with the shocking realization that the sun was all but down and I was standing all alone outside.

When you're a kid, being anywhere outside the well-lit house this time of night was practically a death sentence, and I knew it. Here I stood a slab of fresh meat just waiting for the "Yowl" to pounce on and devour me, bones and all. My fear stoked mind catching spark to the idea that dear old grandpa was doomed to find nothing but a pile of blood soaked, claw rent clothing upon this very spot as he exited the outhouse.

That's when my main spring began winding up, all the while my head spun around trying to look in every direction the "Yowl" might possibly approach from. My only minor consolation being grandpa was a few feet away in the outhouse and Festus was right there at my feet. But in looking down at the ugly little squint eyed Festus, I doubted the protective value of the small dog; besides, he'd acted just as afraid of the "Yowl" as I had. Why else had the little fraidy cat joined us instead of wandering out behind the woodshed as was his habit; and just as my granddad had shook his head contemptuously at me and my fears, so I looked down my nose upon Festus, half dog, half chicken.

Its one thing for a kid to be afraid I thought, but all dogs, even little ugly dogs, should be brave and protective for their masters. After all, didn't caveman domesticate wolves to be used as guard dogs? But then a realization suddenly came to me, "What if the wolves had just been afraid of the dark and huddled up to

The Hair Raising "Yowl"

caveman's fire out of fear? 'Drats' that did shine a whole different light on the already scary situation."

That's when I vowed to myself that if the worse-case scenario happened, "that" being the "Yowl" jumping out and attacking, it was going to be every little dog for himself, for I knew I didn't have to actually outrun the "Yowl", but only outrun Festus. Hence, as the "Yowl" caught and devoured Festus, I would make my escape. I only hoped that poor old grandpa could somehow escape on his own, as the 'Yowl' finished his ugly little squint eye'd dog snack. Such is the bravery of a seven year old amidst the darkness while shivering with fear on the outhouse trail.

Then the outhouse door swung out and grandpa stepped out. Not wanting to be left with my back to the trail unprotected, I shot towards the house, but not too fast. I didn't want to hurry head long into death's clutches, far ahead of grandpa's protection. Therefore, I intermittently shifted into forward and neutral adjusting my speed to meet grandpa's ambling pace towards the house. The whole while, keeping my engine rev'd up ready to shift into high gear at the first sign of anything even remotely close to a "Yowl".

All I can say is, it's a lucky thing for grandpa's back gate that a cricket didn't chirp or a frog croak, for I doubt I could have slowed down enough to actually open such an obstacle, had something sent me into high speed. But just as luck would have it, there wasn't a sound and momentarily we reached the back yard gate.

Stepping inside the yard and within the dimly lit area projected by the back porch light, I shifted into high speed and dashed for the porch door. Immediately abandoning my outhouse compatriots and striking out on my own for sanctuary.

Now, every kid will tell you the most crucial time in avoiding being over taken by a monster is in that split second before you reach safety. Instinctively every kid is hard wired with the knowledge that just inches from safety we are at our most

Archie Matthews

vulnerable from behind. It's that briefest of seconds just before reaching safety that nine out of ten kids are snatched and torn asunder by monsters and/or demons. Of course it's almost impossible to verify these startling statistics with eyewitness accounts, as well you can imagine. You're just going to have to take my word for it.

As I reached out and swung the porch screen door wide, my feet hit the threshold, my every muscle was coiled with the apprehension of being overtaken from behind. Reaching the safety of the well-lit back porch I laid on the breaks and was just beginning to power down my jet engines. When out of the corner of my eye a shadow suddenly appeared from behind the opened freezer door and a scream shattered the evening.

"My goodness!" grandma shouted as she bolted from where she had been leaning into the freezer. "You scarred the life out of me, why in the world did you scream at me like that?"

All I can say is it's a good thing I'd just watered my mule, or he'd have gotten a trough full right then and there on the porch. It was only an entirely empty bladder that kept me from fouling myself and the porch floor that instant as it was. And just as my heart began to beat again, realizing I was still alive and it was only grandma, the screen door banged open and grandpa shouted, "What in the heck is all the screaming about?"

I have no doubt, I lost two years of life in just moments on that back porch, what with all the startling shadows and shouts from my grandparents. Long and short of it, we finally made it into the comfort and safety of the house and settled in for the night. That is to say, grandma and grandpa settled in, while I was still wound up like an over cranked watch spring ready to burst my clockworks at any hint of either a demon and/or monster, let alone another hair raising "Yowl".

I won't bore you with the shaky flashlight climb upstairs to my bed, or the long night of wide eyed, sweat filled, terror. Let's just say, sometime during the night, as usual, I fell unconscious unable to keep my eyes open an instant longer. The next morning as usual, I woke up absolutely amazed I wasn't a pile of bones cast aside by some unknown horror. But once again, I had survived another long night. It now being morning, the sun was shining and I bailed out of bed, got dressed and shot downstairs ready for breakfast, reveling in the fact I had once again survived a night.

Grandma had breakfast ready and on the table waiting for me, so I shoveled it in as fast as I could. This morning I had planned on spending the day down to the blacksmith shop with grandpa, who had long since eaten and been at work at the crack of dawn, hours ago. I was just finishing breakfast when grandma stopped me as I pushed my chair back from the table and was about to head outside.

"Here now, not so fast." She said, "I have some stuff in the kitchen I want you to put out for Bob."

I instantly knew who she meant, for "Bob" was my grandpa's old black and white tom cat. Grandma had been cleaning out the freezer the past couple of days. Each evening she had taken out some of the old dried, freezer burnt, fish that I and grandpa had caught the year before, but we hadn't eaten. That's what she had been taking out of the freezer last night as I had come charging onto the back porch. Now having thawed all night, it was ready to be put in the bowl out in the woodshed for the cat.

I diligently followed grandma into the kitchen and was handed a bowel of smelly dried out, discolored fish. With my face screwed up tight, trying my best not to inhale any of the wafting smelly fish, I set out the back door towards the woodshed.

Festus usually accompanied me outside during the day, watching and snitching on me with his tell-tale bark the moment I began to work up some mischief. But since I had been taking out the smelly fish the past couple of days, he had recently been stopping at the back porch and watched me from the threshold through the low hung screen door, the lazy little mutt. Part of his hesitation might also have been, he was not particularly fond of Bob the tom cat, for although they didn't actually fight like cats and dogs, their standing "Truce" was at best, a bit shaky.

I walked from the back porch to the woodshed and couldn't help but ignite the slow burners on my escape rockets and wind up my main spring just in case.
To a kid scared to death of the dark, the woodshed was a place to be particularly wary of, even during day light. I always played things real careful when dealing with dark and spooky places, and the woodshed was just that type of place.

I eased up to the large rough sawn plank door and lifted the latch. I then carefully stepped back with the door as it swung open towards the outside, carefully keeping the wooden barrier between me and whatever might be inside. Although the outside was full daylight, I knew the inside of the woodshed was dark, and I didn't want to risk being grabbed from some monster lurking in that darkness. Better to allow the light to permeate and cleanse the inside of any lingering demon presence or other dark inhabitant.

Every kid knows light, any kind of light, but especially daylight, evaporates monsters in their tracks. Vampires, demons, zombies, mummies, even Frankenstein as tough as he is, can't withstand sunlight. Everyone knows this, especially a kid well versed on the terrors of the dark as I was. Being such a kid, I knew that by exposing an area to daylight, "Poof" no monsters. The only problem with this scientific fact was that every dark spooky place, such as the woodshed, had pockets of remaining shadows; shadows that always seem to elude the sunlight through the door and remain dangerous and suspect to hiding one horror or another. Lingering shadows can be even more dangerous than darkness, for many a kid has lowered his guard, only to be taken by surprise and fall victim to a "Snatch and Grab". This is when a vile creature thrusts its arm or hooked appendage out from a dark shadow and snatches a tender morsel to be dragged screaming to his death, back into the dim abyss.

The Hair Raising "Yowl"

I had been fairly well versed by television as to the habits of monsters, for I'd snuck on occasion and peered around the hall corner, while mom and dad had watched more than one late night horror episode. I had also stayed the night a time of two with older cousins, who had taken every occasion to explain all kinds of kid snatchings and demon devouring's that had taken place in our neck of the woods. The puzzling thing was how all the adults vehemently denied the existence of Monsters yet would "matter of factly" admit they believed in demons. My older cousin Jimmy had explained it as some kind of "Spell" monsters had over parents that allowed the monsters to snatch kids without the parents even believing in such. Jimmy even told me that I'd had older brothers at one time, but they'd been eaten long ago, before I was even born, and no matter how vehemently I tried to get the truth out of my folks or other relatives, adults would just deny it.

Oh, how I had pleaded many a time that someone would see the reasoning of it and cut several windows into that shadowy building. But suggest as I might in my own subtle way, every time I tried to talk reason with grandpa and describe the dangerous dark corners, he would just look at me like I had a "bat loose in my belfry". And therefore I soon came to realize, I would forever have to remain wary of the shadowed recesses of the woodshed, if I was to avoid a "Snatch and Grab" ending.

As I pulled the door wide, I very carefully peered around it and inside the dimly lit interior. Although I saw the cats dish just inside and to one side of the door, I was carefully looking around towards the two most likely places for monsters to linger. The dark and forbidding coal bin was to the left inside of the woodshed, for even though it was called a woodshed, the stove had been converted to coal, hence, the coal bin.

The coal bin was a huge room into itself that stretched from floor to almost ceiling with a large opening to the front fit with large wooden slats that opened into a small box. The slats could be adjusted to allow the coal to fall forward into the box to be scooped up with the coal bucket. That boxed opening although usually full of coal, often allowed space enough between box and slats for a dark open void to occur. This black void was extremely suspect and I had surmised, might even allow an unknown horror to "Snatch and Grab" an unsuspecting kid. It was an opening that had always given me great pause for thought and today was no different. Therefore, I gave it a good once over and was assured that the coal was pushed down and no black open space was available for vile creatures hooked appendages to shoot through. Satisfied that I needn't worry about terror springing out at me from that direction, I then trained my gaze towards the opposite side of the interior.

To the right of the doorway was another wall with a huge rough sawn door that led into the old cooler, but that heavy door remained shut. Therefore no lurking monsters from that ominous opening, my eyes immediately slid up to the loft above.

The loft above the old cooler was where huge blocks of ice used to be stored in piles of sawdust, so that their evaporation and the resulting cold air would fall down and cool the inside of the well-insulated room below, thus called the "Cooler". Grandma had explained that had once been their "refrigerator" many years ago before the modern invention of the indoor appliance we called a refrigerator.

Grandma had told me the stories of how they used to travel way up to Sage Hen reservoir in the middle of winter and using huge crosscut timber saws cut enormous blocks of ice and brought them home. The whole thing sounded barbaric to me, just short of living in a cave, for she had also explained back in those days, they didn't have any lights other than candles and coal oil lamps. Simply barbaric, I had thought....

I'd often wondered how any kids at all had survived being eaten by monsters back in those days, I imagined they fell in droves. Many times I dwelt on the theory this must be why my dad was so fearless. After all, anyone actually surviving to adulthood without a night light or even a handy flashlight must have been in some mighty hair raising, life or death encounters with all manner of horrors growing up. My reasoning brought me to the conclusion that being one such survivor, my dad must be one tough character. Therefore, many was the scary night I ran to his side seeking safety as a child, as I am sure he will attest.

Recognizing the loft was high enough even the longest armed Demon couldn't reach down and snatch me, I stepped inside and dumped the dried lump of mummified fish into Bob's bowl and quickly eased backwards keeping my eyes to the front to cover my retreat. Keeping one's eyes to the front while backing out of a potentially deadly situation is also a well-known survival tactic every kid uses.

Children understand no monsters hooked appendage will come shooting out if you're diligently watching; it's one of those unspoken truths every kid is instilled with upon birth. Even the deadliest monster or demon, doesn't just jump out at you, but rather sneaks up from behind, or "Snatch and Grabs" you while you're not looking. Thus, easing out backwards and reaching the full sunlight outside, I quickly closed the huge heavy door and let the latch slip into place.

"Ha ha!" I congratulated myself. Once again I had entered into the lion's den and survived. I had triumphantly emerged, safe and sound. All my appendages intact, nothing ripped from its socket and/or devoured. I was a hero, likening myself to such legendary greats as Daniel Boone, Pecos Bill, dad and even grandpa....at least in my own mind, for I had braved the darkness and in doing so had risked being devoured by all kinds of monsters. (Okay, so it was fairly light, but to a kid, there had been some darkness and therefore the possibility of a harrowing death, no matter how remotely.)

Having delivered the stinky cat food, I returned grandmother's bowl, and had spent the rest of my day tinkering in the shop with grandpa; and as so very often happens to a kid on summer school break, the day flashed by in a brief instant, and the long lingering terror filled evening loomed.

Archie Matthews

To a kid, days were bright light filled delights that never lasted long enough, while nights were long seemingly everlasting affairs full of quivering with the blankets up around our ears and the pillow over our heads. Night after night is spent with only our eyes poking from beneath, trying our best to fend off the darkness filled terrors by staying awake.

That evening once again found us sitting out on the front porch after dinner, but this time I was ready for the twilight. I had gone right out after dinner and "watered my mule" as grandma so eloquently put it, while there had been plenty of light to evaporate and or hold off what ever had "Yowled" the evening before.

Don't get me wrong, even in the late afternoon sun shine, I had kept an ever vigilant watch. My escape rockets pilot lights burning ever at the ready to ignite and blast off at the first sound of the "Yowl". For even in the daylight the "Yowl" had my nerves on edge and just the loud squeak of grandpa's dining room chair had made me jump a foot out of my chair at dinner.

Therefore, I was sitting on the porch bannister confidently playing with a pair of green plastic toy soldiers when grandma made the announcement.

"Almost bedtime, best go water them mules", she had suggested, without even looking up from her knitting. It's always amazed me that adults can order children to march to their doom, without even looking up from their delightful pastimes. Many was the time that my own parents ordered me to bed without so much as turning off the TV or singing a death dirge as I marched off, never expecting to see them or daylight again. Yet, only with my expertise at avoiding being a monsters morsel, did I survive, no thanks to them and their scoffing at my nightly battles in the darkness.

Hearing my grandmother's non-chalant orders for me to march off to the gallows,

The Hair Raising "Yowl"

I just smiled and said, "Already did, right after dinner".

Grandpa just grinned, for he knew I was a kid that took approaching evening with the caution it deserved. He'd witnessed by cautious trek out and back to the outhouse and had recognized right off, why I had so willingly sought to water my mules while there was still plenty of daylight left. Grandpa was a man that noticed things.

"Better go again, just to be sure." Grandma quipped.

The evil little Festus lifted his head and hearing the mules needed watered, jumped to his feet and took off around the house, just to show me up. For evidently the stupid little dog had all but forgotten about the hair raising "Yowl" the night before and showed no hesitation about taking back up his evening ritual of visiting his spot out behind the woodshed.

"Festus is off watering his mule, you better go try again", grandma insisted.

"If I water them mules anymore, they'll be dead for sure come morning. I all but turned my insides out, emptying them before." I whined. I had even forgone drinking any and all liquids at dinner, just in case, to be marched off to my doom with an empty bladder? It wasn't going to happen, at least not without a lot of feet dragging and a whole lot of whining.

It's one thing when a guy is sent to water his mule and risk death with a full bladder, but an entirely different thing all together to be ordered into the slavering jaws of a "Yowl" without a drop to be watered, nor a mule to actually drink it. And I wasn't about to march off to what I felt was nothing short of murder should I be forced to go, without some genuine complaining. Therefore, I complained and heartily.

Grandpa chuckled and continued chewing and spitting his tobacco as grandma worked her knitting. "Okay, but remember, it's easier to go before bed, than get up in the middle of the night and go outside." Oh, but those were cryptic words to hear, and I wished I had given them a bit more heed, but once again, that's another story for a later date. I will just say, many a time in the distant future I would come to remember those words, but usually too late.

We sat there for a time enjoying our evening each to our own. Grandma knitting the mysterious yarn pile into whatever it was she happened to be making at the time. While grandpa fiddled with one of the many gadgets that enthralled him throughout the years as he sat and chewed his tobacco. And having been paroled from having to march to the outhouse gallows and water my mule, I sat on my usual perch there upon the front porch bannister with a smile of satisfaction that was instantly cut short by another hair raising "Yowl!"

As with the night before, everyone sat bolt upright with hearing the "Yowl" and then instantly jumped to their feet hearing a loud "YIP" from no other than Festus. I don't know what passed through grandma and grandpa's mind, but I was sure we'd just heard the last of old Festus, for I had no doubt he was deep in the gullet of the "Yowl".

But it was not to be, for a half second later around the corner and up the step, like a bolt of lightning, flashed Festus as if the devil were right on his tail. This immediate arrival of the panting little pooch suddenly appearing, once again made everyone nearly jump right out of our skins.

Reaching the porch, Festus launched and went airborne, his trajectory perfectly timed as grandma opened and closed her arms, expertly catching the little rascal in midair. Then realizing he was now untouchable by whatever it was behind him, he began to bark furiously. Grandpa also began to make barking noises, but I quickly realized he was trying to cough up some of his chewing tobacco that had slipped into his airway.

After several minutes grandma finally got Festus settled down and he stopped barking. And just as quickly grandpa got his tobacco back where it was supposed to be and spit into his awaiting spittoon beside his chair. We stood there for a few minutes more listening intently trying to figure out where and what might have once again made the frightful noise. But it was useless for listen as we might we didn't hear anything and soon decided to call it a night as the sun had set.

We went inside and began to get ready for bed. Grandpa was as usual, the first in bed, grandma closing and locking doors, while I trudged upstairs towards my bed my beaming flashlight trembling in my hand. I was at the head of the stairs and only a few feet from the lamp beside the bed, when once again, the night was shattered by an awful hair raising "Yowl".

This time it sounded like it was about two feet from my ear drum and over taking me fast. Upon hearing the hair raising "Yowl", amazingly enough my "escape rockets" ignited without even a preliminary warm up, and I shot downstairs without touching a stair. Instantly arriving at the bottom of the steps I barely escaped being squashed as I slipped through the stair well door, just as grandma was closing it.

As I popped out of the closing crack, unsuspecting grandma gave a startled scream and Festus began barking furiously once again as pandemonium erupted. Instantly grandpa was up and charging through the bedroom door in nothing but his long john bottoms and a tee shirt ready to battle whatever had suddenly attacked.
"What the devil is going on?" he shouted trying to be heard above the barking little dog.

"Did you hear that?!" I screamed. My hair standing on end as yet another loud and mournful "Yowl" sounded once again, melting me into grandma as I clutched her around the middle. "We're doomed!" I myself howled mournfully.

"Oh for crying out loud, you're going to scare yourself and me to death if you keep this up!" grandma cried.

Archie Matthews

Then looking over where grandpa stood, she said, "Archie, that did sound like it was right outside, you better go see what it was."

I'll never forget the look grandpa shot me. To this very day, I suspect if I hadn't been kin, I think he'd have fed me to the "Yowl" right then and there. It wasn't a pretty look by any means, and only later in life when I was married to my first wife, was I ever to see a more blood thirsty gaze.

"Oh for the love of Pete!" grandpa growled, "It's probably just an old screech owl!"

And then once again the "Yowl" sounded but this time, it was the most mournful, long drawn out sound yet, and even grandpa's eyes widened to hear it.
"Okay, that's it, I'm going." He said, and turning around went back into the bedroom and rummaged around for a few minutes, then came out with a large flashlight and a wicked looking long barreled pistol.

"Come on, you're coming too. I want you to see there is nothing to be so afraid of!" and he was looking right smack dab at me.

I was sorely tempted to take the coward's way out and roll my eyes to the back of my head and pass out, but I couldn't bring it off with such short notice. I took one look at grandpa's eyes and knew short of instantly falling over dead right then and there, I was doomed, and therefore I had to accompany grandpa out and into the darkness.

We went to the back porch and were just opening up the back screen door to the outside when once again a loud long mournful "Yowl" sounded from directly ahead. If I hadn't been between grandpa in the front and grandma standing close behind me, I'd have bolted…to this day, I don't have a clue as to direction, but anyplace would have been better than right there at that moment. That's what accumulated, piled high fear will do to a kid, and I was in way over my head and knew it.

The Hair Raising "Yowl"

"That came from the woodshed", grandpa said. "You stay right behind me, no matter what. Don't step around me and get between this shoot'n iron and whatever that "Yowl" is."

If I hadn't been so utterly terrified, I'd have laughed at the very thought of a herd of wild horses struggling to drag me to the front of this doomed expedition. If I hadn't been in such utter shock at even being in the rear, I'd have chuckled at the thought, but all I can suggest is I was beside myself with fear. So we proceeded down that back sidewalk towards the looming woodshed. Every step taking us farther and farther from the beloved porch light, ever closer to the "Yowl".

"Oh", how I envied grandma as she closed the screen door behind us and stood there watching us edge our way towards the looming dark woodshed.

Grandpa grasped the latch and flung the door open with a mighty jerk and leveled both flashlight in one hand and deadly shooting iron in the other, ready to take on all comers. A half second slipped by and realizing we weren't being devoured as of yet, I slowly peered around grandpa to look inside.

If that woodshed had been spooky during the day, with its few dark corners, it was an utter demon's haven now, with its inky blackness. If that had been my flashlight, I would have scraped it immediately for a better one. Its pitiful beam of light was way too narrow for my tastes. Of course anything short of a Hollywood search light would have been deemed insufficient for me at that point, but it would have been much more appreciated to say the least.

Grandpa slowly moved the flashlight around from the coal bin to the cooler and was just easing the light to the loft when the night was once again shattered by the "Yowl". But this time it was right on top of us, and sounded as if a air raid siren had cut loose announcing another full scale World War and all hell was about to break loose.

Archie Matthews

Upon suddenly hearing the hair raising "Yowl" and so close to hand, World War Three immediately ensued, cannon's, bomb's bursting, screaming, small arms fire…..more screaming….mass hysteria.

What actually took place from that moment on has been a matter of contention within my family for many years.

My grandfather argued with anyone and everyone for years, that his shooting hand had been savagely bumped and that's why his pistol had gone off.
And of course grandma's pointing out "It went off more than once," always seemed to annoy him greatly, especially since it was a "Single action" pistol; that and the fact "That a single action had to be cocked each and every time before pulling the trigger," or so, many people familiar with firearms were always pointing out.

I knew better than to add that his pistol had held six rounds, besides all a person had to do was count the six bullet holes in the back wall of the woodshed to know that. But I realized right off, that grandpa was excitable when the subject of that night was brought back up, so I usually just sat quiet when it was mentioned. (Mostly).

Another huge matter of contention was how I and my granddad had ended inside the woodshed sprawled on the dirt floor. Grandpa forever insisted he'd been pushed from behind and since I was the only one behind, it must have been my fault. But I can assure everyone, and often did, I was in no state of mind to be pushing forward, and am amazed to this day, anything could have dragged me inside. What with my legs churning dirt like a dragster burning rubber off the starting line, trying my best to come in first place safe back at the house.

I can only surmise, somehow grandpa drug me down with him as we crumpled inside, both of us looking directly up into the rafters at the well-lit back end of a hunched up constipated cat, as it

The Hair Raising "Yowl"

once again let out a mournful "Yowl" in its endeavor to relieve itself of the mummified remains of last year's freezer burnt fish.

I for one had not seen the humor in facing the winking one eyed "Yowl", my grandpa had, for I didn't stick around. Since I hadn't the experience to recognize the back end of a constipated cat for what it was, I had only seen an evil winking pink eye amidst a black and white patch of fur.

Needless to say, the untangling of arms and legs had not been a gentle affair, but had involved plenty of flailing on my part, as I set my arms and legs in motion trying my best to break the sound barrier on my way to the safety of the house and grandma. I am ashamed to say; I was forced to abandon my hysterical grandfather to his fate as he lay there like some kind of willing sacrifice, laughing death square in the face. Little did I realize it just so happened to be the other end he was laughing at.

It was upon approaching the back screen door at nearly the speed of sound and seeing what appeared to be grandmother holding the door tightly shut with a look of terror etched on her face; I instantly realized I was being hotly pursued by the winking one eyed "Yowl".

After a milli-second of thought and reaching the conclusion that grandpa had already been devoured, and only the echoes of his laughing remained bouncing around in the dark woodshed, and the "Yowl" was in hot pursuit, I liberally applied the gas to my jet engines and accelerated myself towards the back screen door.

Split second decision making is another trait that terrified children are imbued with as a means of survival, and instantly perceiving the only way of getting inside the house before the winking one eyed "Yowl" caught me, was through the screen at the bottom of the door. Therefore without a moment of hesitation, through the screen I went in a tangle of arms and legs, my tonsils blaring.

Archie Matthews

Thus, the rise of the third and final point of argument that was also heatedly debated for years to come;

Grandma would contend for years, that she had been preparing to open the screen door for me. All the while, with the same breath, vehemently deny, she had mistaken the shadowy form that shot out of the woodshed for anything other than me, her beloved grandson.

But grandpa would incessantly tease her about the same terrifying look I had witnessed, and point out, "It's mighty hard to push a door open, when you're leaning back with all your weight, with your feet braced on either side of the door jamb." And then he would begin laughing and add, "It might have been that strange door opening stance that gave you such trouble getting the door opened quicker."

The one thing that everyone did agree on about the events of that summer involving the hair raising "Yowl"; Once grandma stopped feeding poor old Bob the cat that dried, freezer burnt fish,(which was immediately), the "Yowl" disappeared, never to be seen nor heard from again.

Good thing too, for I and Festus both were on edge the rest of the summer, and needless to say, when we were startled, everyone was affected, one way or another. I just couldn't have gone on living with the constant threat of a prowling "Yowl" any longer. I can't begin to express how overwhelmingly relieved I was when grandpa announced the "Yowl" mystery was not only solved, but had been taken care of.

Not to mention the relief poor old Bob the cat must have felt, after having consumed as much mummified fish as he was able to hold....and hold...and hold.... that long summer.

Furthermore, no matter who tried to convince me otherwise, it wasn't until much later in life, that I actually came to believe the real identity of the hair raising "Yowl".

The Hair Raising "Yowl"

It was only many years into my adulthood, when I was married to the woman that was to bear me two children that I again heard such a "Hair Raising YOWL!" And that's why I broke out into maniacal laughter at that place and time recalling the one eyed winking monster.....and how I came to have a black eye when I stepped out of the hospital birthing room, holding our first and then years later our second born.

But that's another story.....

Archie Matthews

The Hair Raising "Yowl"

The Henchman

When I was a wee tyke one of my role models was my great grandpa Matthews. The man was so remarkable he had defied time, by living to about three hundred years old, by my recollection, but of course at the age of six, what gray haired adult isn't hundreds of years old?

Great grandpa lived in a single room log cabin for as long as I can remember located at the farthest most northern end of my grandpa's blacksmith shop. He had constructed that cabin with his own two hands, which in itself was a miraculous feat, for most people I knew used chain saws and hammers and nails and such, but not my great grandpa. I had heard many people in the family as well as in town say just that, "Old man Matthews built that cabin with his own two hands!" There you go, if that doesn't prove it to you, nothing will. As a small boy, it was enough for me, for over that summer vacation with my grandparents I was to get to know my great grandpa as every small boy should, for the amazing man he was.

Now great grandpa was as I said earlier "Ancient". Just how old he was back then, I can't say, what I can say is the old fellow was the oldest man for miles around and everyone referred to him as "Grumps". He was my dad's grandpa and my grandpa's dad and therefore he was our namesake, "Archibald Matthews the Third". His father had been the second and his grandfather had been the first. The "First" being when his father's brother, being the first boy of the first boy, had died young and without an heir to carry on the family name. So the second son had named his first born "Archibald Matthews" thereby continuing on the long family tradition, but along a different family tree "Branch".

In our long line of generation after generation stretching back when ore was discovered and fire was realized as a means of refining, there has been an Archie in the family and has been a blacksmith in one form or another.

Way back in the beginning they called it copper and then bronze and then iron and ultimately steel, and as in the beginning, there was an Archie and then the last names came about and there became Matthews. Over the years middle names soon came into play and every oldest son of the oldest son was called Archie and Matthews. The difference being that every individual carried his own distinct middle name. My great grandfather's name was Archibald Benjamin Matthews, and his son, my grandfather was Archibald Charles Matthews and my father's

The Henchman

name is Archibald Harry Matthews and my name is Archibald Marton Matthews and my son's name. Well it was once Archibald Matthews as well, but since that person no longer exists, our line must take another branch it seems. But that's another story, albeit a sad one filled with deceit and treachery that we won't go into here.

As with the following line of Archie's, "Grumps" was a blacksmith for as many years as he could swing a hammer. He had established the blacksmith shop in Ola, Idaho and had worked it for many years until one day he turned it completely over to his son, my grandpa. This is where I for as far back as I can remember, I was given the greatest gift imaginable and allowed to spend the summers with my grandparents and for a while "Grumps".

Now, as my aging parents hear my stories, they always look across the room at one another and smile with twinkling eyes as I remark about the magnificent gift they allowed me every year. Little did I know until just recently, they were sharing a joke on me, for all those years I had believed I was the one getting the vacation of a lifetime, while it was my parents that were truly enjoying a magnificent vacation!

I don't have a clue why everyone called my great grandpa "Grumps", although he was often known as "Blunt" and "Opinionated"; he wasn't ever what I'd consider "Grumpy", oh, until that one day, so many years ago. And then "Boy howdy", did that old man fly off the handle....but, after you've heard my story, you decide whether or not he was justified.

Everyone that knew my great grandfather admired the man and respected him, even those that run afoul of him, soon learned he was a force to be reckoned with, even at his vast age. But no one ever claimed he wasn't honest nor forthright, he treated people fair and with an even hand. Oh, sure, there was a time or two his judgment might have been a bit clouded, especially when it came to someone threatening one of his grandkids, or in my case, great grandsons.

Archie Matthews

That summer began like the previous summer, with my parents driving me up to my grandparents in Ola, Idaho. This summer I believe I was six years old and had just been released after my first year stint in the local educational lock up known as Grandview Elementary School. I remember my exuberance at the very beginning of the year to be going to school for the first time. I also remember coming home after that very first day, with my head hung low and everything else dragging behind, including my exhausted backside. So when I say I was excited to be paroled, let alone arrive at my grandparents, you can imagine my exalted happiness.

My folks had stayed the night and then loaded up my baby brothers and disappeared down the road in a cloud of dust, leaving me behind for the next three months. I could say, that even then, my mind was whirling with excitement as to the adventures I knew I was going to have, but I am afraid that might be used by family members as an "Admission of Guilt" and held against me. Therefore I will just say, I was happy and decided to run along and visit "Grumps".

As had been drilled into my head, okay, not actually "Drilled", but surely "Pounded", for in the past if I didn't tell my grandmother where I was going, I certainly got a pounding afterwards. With this in mind, I ran back into the house and asked grandma if I could go see "Grumps"? Grandma agreed but with the warning, "Be a good boy and don't get Grumps all stirred up." So away I went down the walk and out the front gate and making a hard right went north past grandpa's blacksmith shop, to the little wooden cabin at the far end.

As I approached I saw "Grumps" already out on the little roughhewn log porch sitting in his rocking chair. I slowed my pace to an easy walk, for I had "Stirred" up the old man in the past by just running up to his porch. That time he'd given a shout of surprise and quickly produced an old horse pistol as big as a Howitzer cannon and scared the dickens out of me and himself. His shout of surprise being what scared me, his huge

The Henchman

pistol appearing out of no-where and going off is what scared him the most, or should I say, going off and taking a chunk out of his boot tip.

That instance with the pistol scared more than just the two of us, for grandma and grandpa hearing the "familiar" sounding shot of the huge cap and ball pistol, had come running. There had been a lot of "Adult" talk, none of which I had been allowed to partake of, let alone listen in. But it had taught me a valuable lesson concerning Grumps. He was not a man that startled well or as everyone around me called it, "Stirred up".

There wasn't a person for miles around that didn't know Grumps had been a handy man with a pistol away back when. In fact, he'd been a sheriff for several years and had rode the lone trails delivering mail to the scattered small towns north of Boise. More than once Grumps had been faced with trouble and he and his huge pistol had always come out the other side.

Last years "Accidental Shot" had produced quite a rise out of my grandma, and I remember hearing her and grandpa discussing the matter through the floorboards while I was in bed upstairs as they were in their bed directly beneath that very night.

"Archie, Grumps is getting too old to be carrying around that big old pistol anymore.....I'm afraid he's going to accidently hurt someone if not himself." Grandma had said.

"Now Clara, he's carried that pistol for over sixty years. I'm not going to go take it away from him.....and I wouldn't want to see anyone try it, that's when you might see someone hurt. He'll be fine....." and then I must have fallen asleep or that was the end of it, for I never could remember the rest, if there was any.

So I had learned not to "Stir up" Grumps, as everyone would tell you, that knew the old boy, when he got stirred up, pretty much everyone in a wide radius became suddenly embroiled in the same stew pot and everyone and everything seemed to get stirred....but not all up, for more than once, someone ended

Archie Matthews

getting "Stirred Down". But it was a well-known fact it was best to just leave Grumps, the little old man at the end of town, alone, which most people gladly did.

That's why I'd slowed my hurried pace and cautiously approached Grumps as he sat quietly rocking on his front porch. Easing up to the old cabin I slowed my pace to almost a crawl and said in a normal tone, so as not to shout, "Hey Grumps……it's me, I'm back for the summer!" and I stopped for a minute to let his old eyes adjust and focus on me.

For a few seconds the old fellow squinted and twisted up his face as if he were trying to see through a keyhole full of cobwebs. "Who the heck are you?" he shouted, "What the heck are you whispering about? What are you, some kinda injun? Have you come sneaking up on a poor old man to lift my hair? You dern smart alecky kid! Where's my dog…I'm gonna sic him on you!" the old fellow ranted and began shaking his crooked willow cane at me.

Talk about suddenly shifting my forward gear into neutral, which wasn't hard, for I was barely moving forward to begin with. But hearing my great grandpa not even recognize me, stopped me in my tracks, and realizing he was shouting and apparently had become hard of hearing if not entirely deaf, shocked me to a standstill. Then to make things even worse, I suddenly realized the old boy had finally slid off his rocker, and I don't mean his chair, by thinking he still had a dog.
At that moment you could have knocked me over with a stiff breeze, until a second later he smiled and began to laugh and threw open his arms.

"Ah, Grumps! You were fooling me!" I laughed as I ran up the steps and ran into his awaiting hug.

"HA, I got you for a minute, you thought like the rest of these fools around here, your old Grumps was a few bricks shy of a full load….Well I'll tell ya what! I can see fine, and hear fine and if 'n I had a dog, he'd be a real sic'em!" Grumps laughed.

188

The Henchman

"You got me. But I didn't think about any bricks?" I laughed a bit puzzled.

"Ah, never mind. So how you been keeping yourself? Did you learn lots in your first year of school?" he asked as he held me out at arm's length and smiled.

"Blah, I hate that school. Way too many rules and girls everywhere. Do this and don't do that. My teacher hates me." I groaned.

"Yup, but what did you learn this year?" Grumps asked patiently, "Did you learn to count? Did you learn your numbers....Did you learn your letters?"

"Well, I learned to hate school, I can tell you that! Yes, I learned numbers and some letters, but I can't spell good", I assured the old fellow.

That's when we were both distracted by a loud rumbling, rattling sound accompanied by faint "barking", and Grumps said, "Well, sounds like the village idiot's a come 'n.....you best stay up here on the porch, I doubt even that fool will run us over while we're up here, although ya never know about him."

Grumps had a definite dislike for "George Wellner" for that's whose old blue, smoke belching truck came around the far corner, up on two wheels and racing down the road. That truck was in and out of town so fast, if you'd have blinked you might have missed it, which was hard not to do, because of the eye watering black smoke that came belching out of it.

As the old truck sped by, all but obscured by a dense black cloud, the rattling was almost deafening, or would have been if it could have been heard over the deafening "barking" coming from the thousand and one dogs piled in the back. Okay, there wasn't quite a "Thousand and One dogs", but most people agreed it was a lot of dogs, and therefore most just referred to it as the

Archie Matthews

"Herd of dogs". Being six, I couldn't count to a Thousand yet, but I also couldn't count high enough to individually itemize the "Herd" either, so mostly I just claimed it was a "Thousand and one". To my defense, I'd offer if you've ever laid eyes on an entire pickup bed full to the brim of barking, baying and howling dogs of every size, shape, color and breed, you'd think it was a Thousand and one too.

The truck roared out of town and up the little hill and just as it exited town, the door to the café across the street opened up and several people came rushing out. A few of the unwitting strangers stood for a brief moment on the café' steps, while the locals, including the owner and his wife, Eddy and Elaine, both quickly crossed the street and stood in front of the blacksmith shop. There they began shouting and motioning for the unknowing tourists to abandon the steps of the café and come across the street where it was safer.

And then here came old Ed Shotz the store owner who happened to be in the café at the time and hurried up on Grumps porch. Ed being one of Grumps oldest surviving friends stepped up on the porch and gave me a smile and me a hair tussle, then Grumps a friendly nod.

"I got two bit's says the nut piles her up this time and sends that café, gas pumps and all to the moon!" Ed said, as we watched the old truck exit town and head for the small hill at the edge of town.

"You're on!" Grumps gleefully shouted as he shook his old twisted willow cane in his hand and gave me a sly wink, "And I'll foot the bill to fill in the hole for both the Nut and the Café!"

The loud blue truck had stopped belching smoke as it began to ascend the small hill at the end of town, and then it slowed down and came to a rolling stop at the very top. It lingered there for a brief second and as it stopped ever so briefly, so did the barking of the dogs. Then the truck began to slowly roll back downhill and as it began to move once again, the dogs began barking

The Henchman

furiously again. But now the old blue truck was rolling backwards directly lined up with the café's gas pumps.

"Sure enough, he's got her lined up this time Eddy!" someone shouted from the little crowd, and after a brief moment another shout broke forth, "She's gonna blow for sure this time!"

I stepped up to the old twisted tree limb that had been whittled and shaped into Grumps porch rail and looked down towards the blacksmith shop at the crowd of people standing there. Eddy and Elaine both had looks of doom and destruction written across their faces as they watched the old truck rolling backwards towards their home and business. Meanwhile several others were smiling broadly including grandpa, for this was not the first time this scenario had played out.

Grandpa always came out of his blacksmith shop as did almost everyone in town, to see the sight as "Old George" came to town. It was well known that old George's truck had no breaks, regular or emergency, therefore he always cut the motor and rolled to the top of the little hill outside of town and then came rolling backwards towards the café. All the locals knew this, but the visitors hadn't a clue, but were being quickly informed of the situation by either Eddy or Elaine. For they had shouted at the first sign of "Old George" coming to town, to "get outside and run for their lives!", I know because I'd been in the café a time or two when the alarm had been given and everyone had been hustled outside.

Now everyone was watching the old blue pickup rolling backwards directly in line with the two gas pumps. And then just as everyone hunched their shoulders and began to wince at seeing and hearing, let alone feeling a massive explosion, the blue pickup suddenly swerved and missed the pumps. Just as the truck missed the pumps, out jumped a stout looking snow white haired old man and running quickly to the back of the truck, he dropped the tailgate.

Archie Matthews

If you watched the stranger's faces, which I always did, you could see the different emotions of first disaster and then shock as the truck missed the pumps. Then you could see the puzzlement suddenly appear as it looked like the little old man had grabbed one of the thousand and one dogs that were still baying and barking in the back. Then you'd see their faces twist in horror as they saw the old white haired dog abuser, throw something under the back wheel. And as if to punctuate his intense hatred and art full disposal of a couple of the mutts, he'd grab another and throw it in front of the wheel stopping it and keeping it from rolling forward.

Once in a while, a woman would faint, or you'd see one of the city folks lose the lunch he'd been eating or had just eaten over to the café, but most times the strangers realized they weren't dogs thrown under the wheel, but a couple of big rocks.

And then as if on cue, everyone would shout and jump up and down and celebrate nobody had been blown to smithereens, or in the strangers cases, no dogs had been squished flat, either way, everyone especially Eddy and Elaine were happy as could be.

Grumps also gave a loud shout, but not for the same reason as everyone else, for he despised "old George" and let everyone who'd listen know it. Nope, he'd have gotten an even bigger hoot out of seeing old George blow himself up, but he'd have lost his wager with Ed, not to mention had to pay for filling in the holes. Grumps believed a bet was a bet and a man's word was a testament that was to be upheld "no matter what!" Grumps was currently celebrating winning his bet and was dancing around and waggled his old crooked cane in Ed's face.

"Cough it up, you old tightwad! That'll be two bits!" he cackled and held out his hand.

"Well, it's bound to happen one of these times. The old fools had a good run, but he'll misjudge one of these days and 'BLAM!' up she'll go.....and more than likely, he'll take you and your porch with him." Ed said with a teasing smile as he handed over the quarter and placed it in Grumps open hand. "If'n I was you, I'd mend my ways and get right with the man upstairs, especially since your living this close to two thousand gallons of underground gasoline and old George with no breaks."

Of course Grumps just scoffed, "Bah, the Devil don't want that kinda knothead in hell, he'd forget to put wood on the fire and it would go out. Besides, the way I got it figured, George is one of those mill stones about all our necks, and everyone knows mill stones don't blow up, they just sink quietly away."

That gave both me and Ed something to puzzle over, and I still do to this day….and I can honestly say, when old George did finally go, it wasn't to just "sink quietly away", and I don't have a clue which direction he did finally travel, be it heaven or hell; but he went with a "Bang", and it wasn't from blowing up backing over gas tanks either. But that's another story, back to the one at hand.

The next moment the crowd surged back over to the café and past the old white haired George Wellner who stood beside the truck with a huge grin on his face. The strangest part of the whole incident was as the truck's motion stopped and as if a switch had been thrown, the barking suddenly ceased. That once again struck the strangers as odd as ever they had seen, for it was a bit of a spooky thing, if you weren't used to it like me and Grumps and the other locals were. For who trains a huge pack of dogs to suddenly as if by command and in perfect unison, cease barking. As far as anyone knew, and I'd heard a lot of speculation on the topic, nobody knew including old George himself, why them dogs just suddenly stopped, but they always did right on cue as the truck ceased motion.

Ed quickly abandoned the porch and headed back over to the Café to resume whatever he was doing before he was so rudely interrupted, or so he remarked as he went. I began to follow him and headed for the steps, when Grumps third hand snaked around my neck and stopped me dead in my tracks. Well at least my head, my body all but took another step and only with the quick dexterity a small kid possesses did I stay on my feet and not end up on my back. What with Grumps hooked cane handle around my neck, I turned in my tracks and faced my captor.

"Here now, where the dickens are you off to so fast? Hold it thar," he snapped as he'd captured me with his cane handle. "I got an errand for you." He said holding the quarter up for me to see.

"I got Ed's quarter here and he thinks I'm done with him, but I ain't", and he shook the quarter he held betwixt thumb and index finger at Ed retreating back, "I need a henchman", he explained with a crafty smile as he looked back down at me and held the quarter for me to see.

"Well, I was just going over to pet them dogs….but what's a henchman?" I quickly said seeing that shiny quarter about two inches from my nose and Grumps pulled me close with his cane.

"Well a henchman is a partner kind of, but a silent partner…..say like a fellow that might go get a bottle of pop for the other fellow but would keep quiet about it…..Get my meaning?" Grumps said with a squinted left eye and a soul piercing right eye as he leaned down towards me, all the while he held me close with his old twisty cane about the neck.

"But, Grumps….." I began, for we both knew he was NOT supposed to have soda pop. It was some kind of sickness where he wasn't supposed to eat any sugar, and I'd been put on notice to the fact at the end of grandma's switch, more than once, the year before.

"Now don't you but Grumps me…..you ain't one of them 'fraidy cats' er you?! They didn't tell me you'd turned into a yellow girdled girl…..is you my great grandson…or is you my great granddaughter?" he asked with disgust so thick you could have cut it with a knife. Not that Grumps despised females, but the

194

The Henchman

way he figured it, a man had to take risks, especially when a great grandpa needed a soda and there wasn't anyone else for miles around that didn't know better. But he also knew a boy of six that's been raised with only other boys, does despise girls and to even hint at calling me a girl would definitely urge me into all kinds of mischief. Grumps was a crafty old character, many people including my dad and granddad would support the fact by saying "Old Grumps didn't get his age by being a fool….he's a crafty old character." I'd heard it a thousand times from both.

"Okay, but if I get caught it'll be off to the woodshed with me and grandma close behind with her switch." I said as I reached out with the quarter.

"That's what henchman means…..if your caught, you just tell your grandma, I forced you into becoming my henchman…..she won't switch you for that, but don't you tell Ed Shotz your buying me a soda pop, or you'll not get one out of him all summer, for you or for me….he's a dastardly rascal and is in cahoots with the rest of them. They all want to see me live till I'm a thousand years old, miserable and all wore out, but I aim to go out in a blaze of glory! With a dab or two of soda to wet my whistle on the way!" And with that he placed the quarter in my palm and curled my fingers closed with his own.

"Now remember, 'henchman', don't you tell that dern store keep or we'll both suffer a long dry spell. He's a crafty old snake and he'll have it out of you if 'n you ain't sly…..So keep your words short and get your old Grumps a soda. I'm count 'n on you…." And with a deft flick of his wrist, my neck was free again and his cane slid to his side and he sat back down in his rocker and began riding it like his tail was on fire. Which it very well might have been, for grandma was fond of saying, "That Grumps, ain't far from hell, he keeps horse racing with the devil!"

You could always tell Grumps had something on his mind, grandpa always claimed, for he'd start rocking in his rocking chair so fast, my grandmother claimed if you dropped the butter churn in his lap, you'd have butter in a minute flat. And right now

Archie Matthews

you could tell the old fellow had that soda on his mind as he rested both hands atop his cane between his knees and rocked back and forth staring straight out across space, licking his lips in anticipation.

So down the steps I went and up the street past the shop and then the house and across the little side street that separated the grandparent's house and the general store. I had to step way up on the elevated board walk that ran from this side of the store across its front and to the far side that. The far end dropped a good four feet down to the road that slowly dropped down away from town. People that loaded heavy goods mostly just backed up to that far end of the boardwalk and dropped their tail gates and loaded large barrels and large sacks of goods. This particular end of the boardwalk although much lower to the ground, was still a pretty high step for a short legged kid. I was always more than a bit leery of that other end and it's drop off, for more than once I'd forgot about it until I'd taken a tumble. A four foot drop to a three foot kid seemed like quite a height, especially since that ground below was hard packed from all those farm trucks.

I clattered down the boardwalk at a good trot wanting to hurry and get that soda pop, I was dry and knew good old Grumps would share a draught or two with his favorite great grandson...."The Henchman", for that's how he referred to me all that summer and forever afterwards, through one adventure or another together. Mostly he'd just send me on the adventures, and once in a while when things turned sour, he'd jump in where he was needed, between me and the woodshed, mostly. But as you will see, more than once, he rescued his "Henchman" from more than a switch 'n.

As I approached the door at a quick trot, I walked right into the door. Nope, not "in through" the door, you heard right, I said "Into the door", for I hadn't remembered, Ed had went to the café, and since he was there and not here, he'd closed shop and the front door was locked. Therefore, I'd walked smack dab right into the door...and boy howdy, let me tell you; If I'd been six big

The Henchman

strapping burglar's with crowbars, that store would have been just as safe as it was against one little boy. That door never gave a smidgeon and what with the forward momentum I'd generated, I mashed up against that door as if I'd been dropped from a two story building. Squished almost flat, while I was still standing, and surprising it might be to you the reader, I can tell you, it was mighty surprising to me, when I woke up a moment later, flat on my back on the board walk, feeling just like I'd been dropped from a second story building.

For a moment I wasn't sure what had happened, one minute I remembered going into the store and the next moment I was suddenly waking up stretched out atop the boardwalk. I was just sitting there looking around to see where that second story window was that I'd been pushed out of, when I heard a voice call out, "Are you alright?"; scrambling to my feet and turning about, I saw Ace' Glean standing just inside his yard looking across his fence with a quizzical expression on his face. Ace and Margery Glean owned the large house across Main Street from the general store.

"I'm okay", I replied.

"Ed's out for a bit, say's so there on the door, he won't be long, I'd give him a bit." Ace' called out.

"Thank you!" I said, more than a little embarrassed at having the town's biggest cattleman see me stretched out like some kind of bathing beauty waiting for a suntan. And with that, I quickly headed back up the boardwalk, across the side street and through the grandparents gate. I gave a sigh of relief and shook my head a bit and reaching up with my hand to sooth my aching forehead, I noticed a huge knot right between my eyes.

"Drats!" I moaned, for I knew if grandma saw this bump, I was going to be held accountable for it. Love my grandmother though I did, the woman was the biggest snoop when it came to bumps, bruises, gashes, punctures and broken bones. The woman had some kind of abnormal need to know ever little detail of everything and anything that broke my hide, even when it hadn't broken the hide and only left it either dimpled or bumped. The only time she didn't ever put the screws to me and insist I tell her how I got hurt, was when she was applying the switch to my backside. And brother....let me say, that's the one time I was shouting out the cause to my painful backside, but the little old torturer never heeded my distress much at those little "Shindigs". Her willow would strike up the tune and my legs danced the tune, all the while I was calling out the dosy-dow, but it surely wouldn't have been called a square dance, for my tortured body just naturally ran around in a circle. Of course, grandma was the hub of the circle, her willow the spokes and my backside the outside circumference....and around and around we'd go.

Just the sight of her clutching a fist full of willows set me to spilling my guts. And when your torture subject is telling you everything you need to know faster than you could even formulate questions, let alone ask, where's the need to actually ask them? But let me show up with a bump, ding or dent, and a thousand questions would be thrown at me and I would be examined and cross examined without even my rights read to me, let alone a lawyer appointed.

Then I gave a bit of a smile, for a birds egg it might be, or that's what a knot on the head was referred to by grandma, it hadn't broken the hide. "WooHoo!" I laughed, seeing no blood on my hand.

You the reader might wonder why no blood might elicit a "WooHoo" from me, and it wasn't because I was squeamish of seeing blood. I've never been afraid of seeing blood, although there has been a time or two I was a might concerned at the amount of blood, but not afraid. Being a boy and raised with brothers, we tended to bleed and bleed often. Mostly at the hands of one another while pushing and shoving and all the other minor accidents rambunctious boys encounter.

I had a moment of relief at realizing my hide wasn't breached, which wouldn't have been much of a concern, as long as it was in a concealable location. But smack dab center between my eyes, this was not going to go unnoticed by the medicinal snoop....grandma. No sir'ee, this birds egg, she was definitely going to notice, and once again as my fingers gently roamed over the bump, I counted my blessings, for I could only imagine a scalding hot dab of Mercurochrome being sloshed between the eyes. My whole body winced at the thought of the lava hot liquid that my grandmother so eagerly loved to apply to each and every scratch, scrap, cut or open wound. No matter how much I begged and pleaded, scratched, clawed or eventually down and out right fought tooth and nail, could I get a reprieve from having the liquid lava like antiseptic applied.

Head wounds were always the worst. "Oh sure", just about anywhere was soul searing when a liberal dousing of the fiery red liquid was concerned, but the head always hurt the worse. I figured it was because the head was so close to my brain that the pain didn't have far to travel, not like say, a pinky toe. A pinky toe was my chosen favorite if given a choice for a hide scalding with the fiery antiseptic. Way down there at the body's farthest nether parts was where I'd take every cut, scratch, nick or abrasion if given the choice. It seemed that due to the far off vast reaches of a pinky toe, the pain bearing telegraph message to the brain somehow became a bit diluted and muffled. But a head wound, "WOWZERS!" talk about an instant and loud message of pain to the brain.

"You're on fire! And I'm not talking the other side of town, down the street, or even next door, but you MR. HEAD are on FIRE!" And with that kind of fire alarm service, all hell breaks loose in the body. The brain instantly sends messages to all its allies that it needs "Help!" and they all respond in turn.

First the eyes try their best to water up and extinguish the inferno as does the nose as it opens the flood gates and runs like a river with a mission. Next the mouth begins broadcasting the general fire alarm letting everything and everyone within shouting distance know that the body's on fire. Of course the arms are next to enter into the "fracas" along with the hands. Usually they begin doing their best to repel the fire applicator and failing there, they then revert to trying to smack out the flames. It's this wild flailing that accounts for the beating and slapping at one's own head immediately following a Mercurochrome application. There is usually a lot of confusion associated with this and many has been the spectator that jumped to the conclusion it was some kind of mental fit such as throwing a 'tantrum', but I assure you this is a fire fighting tactic.

The next thing in the body's volunteer fire fighting arsenal is the legs that always seem to kick into the fray about dead last, due to their remote location way down at the farther end of the torso. They immediately try their best to take the entire flame engulfed structure to another location, preferably one with loads of cool heat extinguishing water. But since the brain being awash with excruciating pain, is unable to direct the legs, they usually just run in place or sometimes in a futile circle. Usually the circle is the direct result of the medicinal torturer grabbing my belt loop on my trousers and thereby trotting me in a circle as if she were exercising livestock. This is similar to when a "Switch or belt" applicator grabs you by the arm and begins applying it liberally to ones backside. Many is the woodshed that has this mysterious circle deeply worn into its floor. But the two are not to be confused, and are entirely separate although a bit similar results, the similarity being the immense pain and the differences, well you've probably experienced them and need no further explanation.

It was for all these reasons, that I was so elated to just have the 'bird's egg' between my eyes and not have the hide broken. And just as I was finished patting myself on the back and my arm was coming back around from its twisted congratulations, here came the old medicinal maniac herself and before I knew it, I was ambushed by grandma.

"Well my goodness, where have you been, I've been looking all over for ……" and then I saw that evil glint in her eye as she spotted the birds egg, "Oh my, what have you done to yourself?! Where on earth did you get that bump? When did you do that?

How did this happen?" and then before I could keep my distance, she had me clutched and began poking and prodding.

After being released and pronounced I was going to "Live", I was then told Grandpa wanted me down to the blacksmith shop, and then sent on my way out the side gate towards the back of the shop.

I ran down the outhouse trail and since my bladder had been screaming at the top of my lungs, (you know you're bladders full when it's stretched way up there). I decided since I was right there, I might as well stop, so I did. Remembering this is a family type story, I won't go into detail other than to say, "I watered my mules."

I know, "watering mules" in an outhouse is a very confusing concept, but believe me when I tell you, just get used to the fact, although we had no mules, I evidently watered a pair of them in that little three foot square building and lets just leave it to that. If you want to be even more confused, imagine it as a "Closet that somehow had water in it, and was constantly visited by the female persuasion". And "Nope" there wasn't any water in there, other than what the female took in with her....and that's all I am going to say about that. Like I said, "Confusing", and I dealt with that kind of reasoning my whole life from that side of the family, but still loved them all.

It all stemmed from my delicate grandmothers insistence that "Boys watered their mules" while "Young ladies visited the water closet". Grandma's reasoning was, "Rude little boys go "Pee", while polite little boys, "water their mules". As a kid, I always wondered if her delusions actually went further and she honestly believed, I was watering livestock in the outhouse, or did she actually realize I was a "Rude boy" peeing in there and just lying about the mules, all the while she went along with the chicanery? Like I said, it was enormously confusing and we'll just leave it at that. I can't even begin to talk about "little girls and water closets".

Archie Matthews

Anyways, after relieving my bladder of its "mule water", I ambled on down the trail through the scrap yard towards the shop. I know if you're a female reading this, you and every other female on earth wants to know why boys hold it and hold it until their bladders are screaming?....it's a common question many a female asked me when I was a kid including my mother and both grandmother's, as well as countless female teachers and each time they asked, they received the very same answer, which was a shoulder shrug.

But I tell you now, the real reason every boy invariably exercises his bladder and stretches it to the size of a small waste water lagoon, is this one simple reason. "We as males have too many other things on our minds to be bothered by the girlish pleas of our bodies crying for relief." Depending upon the particular male, that could be a wide variety of things, even now at the age of fifty, I still hold it as long as I can and proceed on with my much more important life duties, tasks, missions and adventures. Ask my wife and she will tell you, many is the time she's seen me suddenly break away from a task to run and water my mules as if my mules were about to fall over dead from lack of water.

In fact, when I was working as a construction worker on the Bonneville Ship Locks bordering Washington and Oregon, my sudden dropping of tools and tool belt and running to relieve myself had caused more than one stampede by my co-workers for high ground. It's strange how easily spooked grown men can become while working down deep in a hole, behind a temporary dam holding back millions of water, yet one guy with a stretched bladder drops everything and runs for the outhouse up on the hillside, and panic can instantly set the herd into a frenzy. Not to mention sending the job superintendent into raging fits. But that's another story.

The real puzzlement is why girls don't hold it and seem to have to "visit the water closet after nearly every sip of liquid? Stick that in your thinking cap and smoke it.....whoops, back to the story before I get myself into trouble. I forget sometimes that my wife, daughters and mother read these stories too.

After a successful "Watering of the mules", not to be confused with the "Running of the bulls", although the fast pace of both events is similar, I made my way through the scrap yard and I knocked loudly then entered the rear door to grandpa's blacksmith shop. I slowly pushed the door inwards careful not to just thrust it open and startle grandpa with a handful of hot iron fresh from the nearby forge.

My dad's younger brother uncle Danny still has a scar from when he was a kid and had run to the door, thrown it wide and ran inside to hide while playing hide and seek. As my uncle immediately found out when he ran into a startled blacksmith quickly turning to see what was happening, complete with a white hot tipped steel rod in his hand. Well, let's just say, Uncle Danny found out real quick a kid accidently set on fire is not at all hard to find. Although my dad is fond of saying "he was a tad bit hard for your grandpa to run down and extinguish before he sat the whole town on fire the way he took off."

I think my dad happened to be "It" and was supposed to be doing the "seeking" that particular day and his enflamed younger brother happened to be found rather quickly, or so the tale goes.

It was this incident that had been repeatedly told to me and retold to me trying their best to get it in my head that a loud knock and careful entry was for my own good. And after my own harrowing experience just last summer of accidently stepping between grandpa's forge and the anvil, I wasn't likely to forget "warnings on how to not get set aflame". I was still counting my blessings for surviving that one, for although grandpa was older now, he was every bit as quick extinguishing kids on fire.

I had been extremely fortunate that day, for I had entered the dark shop from the far end and the front, and not announced my arrival by calling out. Therefore grandpa standing at the fiery forge, intently watching the blazing brightness of the metal for it to get to that precise color he needed, hadn't seen me.

Archie Matthews

I had been told not to step between the anvil and forge a dozen times. It had been explained to me over and over that in looking into that bright flaming forge, a blacksmith, any blacksmith would be unable to see anything other than that bright glowing end of the iron as it's quickly brought to the anvil to be worked. And just as I stepped around the anvil and was trying to see what grandpa had in the forge, he wheeled around with a glowing hot piece of iron.

It amazes me to this day, how fast a shirt bursts into flames when touched by a hot piece of iron. What's even more startling is how fast my aging grandfather dropped that white hot poker, snatched his flaming grandson up and doused me in his slag tank. Three things I realized that day that I never forgot; The first being, it pays to listen to grandparents and parents, especially about how not to catch on fire. The second being, even though a person is old, doesn't necessarily mean they are slow, for my grandfather had hands as quick as any gunfighter. I'd pit him against anyone that even remotely thought they could draw a grandkid from the ground and twirl him in the air and deposit him in a slag tank any faster than he did at the ripe old age of sixty eight years old. He was that fast, so fast, that the only thing that suffered was my pride and that brand new shirt, for I had been extinguished before even my under shirt could scorch. "Boy howdy" that's fast….and if you don't believe me give it a try, but I wouldn't if I was you. That's the stuff nightmares are made of……and once in a while I still have them over the whole incident. The third realization was never ever sneak up on an armed man…..be it hot steel or otherwise. The only problem with this third and last realization is quite often it's hard to know who is armed and who isn't.

Upon entering the shop, I saw grandpa poking his fire and stepped over by the work bench and watched as he expertly hooked and drug out a "Clinker"; a clinker being a glassy porous mass of impurities resulting when the coal turning into coke and burning off while leaving the Clinker behind. With the clinker out of his way, and seeing me waiting patiently like I was supposed to, grandpa smiled and banking his coal fire, came and sat down on his nail keg.

I stepped up close and grandpa began to remind me of "things I needed to remember for all of us to have a nice summer together".

Most were instructions of the common sense kind, which I imagine every kid is reminded of every time they go to their grandparents. Like, no playing with matches, no taking rides from strangers...."especially Old George Wellner".....not that George was a stranger, but as grandpa put it, he wasn't known as the safest driver around. Then we went over the obvious, like don't walk between the anvil and the forge....and with that one I nodded vigorously as grandpa chuckled. Then we touched on a few more, like...."Don't startle Grumps....don't give Grumps candy.....and so on and so forth....there was a whole lot of "don't" and "Grumps". And just as grandpa finished and I was sent on my way with a pat on the head and a "That's a good boy, you go play now and try your best to stay out of mischief ", I heard him call to me before I went out the front door, "and no soda pop for Grumps!" Which all but stopped me half in and half out of the shop door and then just the moment I hesitated, I heard Grumps yell, "I heard that!"

Now I was in for it, for I'd taken Grumps quarter and knew I had to deliver or I was in for it, but I also knew I'd be in for it just as deep, if not even deeper, if grandpa and grandma caught me giving Grumps his soda. I stood in the shop door caught between a rock and a hard place and kept looking back towards grandpa at his forge, and down the long front of the shop at Grumps little front porch where he was still rocking in his chair.

Seeing Ed Shotz come out of the café and walk up the street towards the grocery store caught my fullest attention, and then I heard a "cough" come from Grumps, and I looked down his way to see him watching me intently shaking his old crooked willow cane at me and then point it at the store owner. I knew I had to buck up and get that soda, or else. Oh, don't get me wrong, I

Archie Matthews

wasn't a bit afraid of that kind old man or his cane. He'd yell and shout alright and shake his cane and jump up and down, but I knew he'd have waded into a herd of man eating grizzlies for me. He'd proven that last year, by wading right into three of them just as they were about to devour me.

Last year I'd played a dirty trick on three of Ace's cowboys. Ace had hired the three locals to move his cattle from their winter pastures up to the open range above town in the timber. After they'd accomplished that as they did every year, they all rode their horses into town and went into the Café where beer was served. They'd drank and "Whooped it up" most of the afternoon.

I'd been hanging around the café in hopes of a soda pop hand out or a piece of candy from good old Eddy Mehan, when one of those half drunken cow hands had staggered by and stepped on my toe with his big cowboy boots and I'd pitched a fit. He'd just given me a brush aside and never as much as a "Pardon me". Therefore I'd a "burr" under my saddle, and because he'd placed a proverbial burr under my saddle, I decided I might as well return the favor.

Back in my childhood, I was big on "doing unto others as they did to me…..and sometimes even before they could actually do unto me." As a kid sometimes life just presents "opportunities" to perpetrate upon others ….. This time, I felt thoroughly justified to do unto this big footed cowboy, it just so happened he had a couple of friends that got roped into the same deal. I figured that's what they got for having such a big footed obnoxious friend.

Since the little town of Ola still had a lot of locals that rode horses to town, the general store, the café and grandpa's blacksmith shop all had hitching rails. So it was not uncommon to see horses tied up to any of them at any time of night or day, therefore it wasn't surprising to see these cowboys had tied their horses up to an old hitch rail along the side of the café. And it

The Henchman

was "Providence" that particular side of the café didn't have a window facing that hitching post, nor the horses tied to them.

I'd come out of the café, and immediately set across the road to the little crick that run along the side of Grump's cabin. After a few minutes of searching around, I found just exactly what I wanted and quickly ran back and visited those cowponies. I knew which horse that Kinkaid boy rode, for he'd been the owner of the big foot that had squished my pinky toe, and with that knowledge, I left him and his cronies with my best regards.

After visiting those horses, I'd gone back over and sat on Grump's steps to watch the show and I wasn't waiting long before those three drunken cowboys came staggering out and got on their horses. I couldn't have planned the whole thing any better, for all three had put their boots in the stirrups and hit the saddles at the same time. Nor did I have long to wait as those drunks swung aboard, their saddles came up and met their backsides half way to the saddle, and talk about excitement. One minute it was three drunks ready to ride home and the next it was a full blown "Wild West Rodeo". The burrs under those saddles must have been extra pointy for those horses sure did come alive and show some buck. The first two cowboys pitched and battled and ever time they'd come back down they went up a bit higher the next time, until both of them hit the ground and their horses run down the road out of town, bucking all the way.

But that Kinkaid boy, since he'd been the one I and my pinky toe was really sore at; I'd added a little something extra, in the form of a loosened cinch. You want to talk about as funny a sight as I'd ever seen. That drunken cowboy had both feet firmly into his stirrups and was hanging on to the saddle horn for dear life, as it quickly spun from the top of the horse to the bottom. If you've never seen a cowboy upside down, his stirrups sticking straight up into the air as the bucking bronco goes up and comes down and pile drives the rider right into the ground, you haven't seen anything. About the third time his head hit the ground, I don't know if he was knocked loose or finally had the good sense to just let go, whichever it was, he come out of the saddle and

Archie Matthews

rolled to the side, those four horse's hooves barely missing him on their way down. Then as if the horse realized it had fulfilled the revenge it had been duly assigned, it too galloped off dragging the saddle beneath, rope, saddlebags, broken stirrup flying every which a way as it went.

All I can say is, it was a hilarious sight to everyone that had ran out of the café to see what all the yelling and horse screaming was about, just in time to see everyone bucked off and the Kinkaid boy being pile driven head first into the ground. I suppose they'd have never even thought about me being implicated, if I hadn't been the loudest one of the bunch, for I was shouting encouragement to those horses, all the while I was jumping up and down laughing my head off and slapping my knee for all I was worth.

Getting to their feet and watching their horses run off, the Kinkaid boy lay where he'd fallen holding his sore head just like I'd held my sore toe. And I was laughing and relishing my revenge as was my abused pinky toe, when three pair of evil eyes swung over my direction and with a shout here they come.

Being a kid, I hadn't given thought as to my position until those three angry young men come across the street, and there I was cornered atop a boxed in porch. I suddenly wished I'd have given more thought to an escape route as I had the actual "Burr under the saddle" idea, but I hadn't and it looked like I was going to get a thrashing. Well, even though I was only five back then, I'd been raised to stand fast and was bound and determined to give as good as I got, although the way I figured it, they were going to get the meal, while I was just going to get a bite and more like a nibble. But I was determined to get my bite in, and so there I stood and watched them come.

I have to say, they was mighty brave men in their early twenties, for all three of them came up the steps together, and wasn't showing the least bit of fear of me, their lone five year old adversary. I remember balling up my fists and getting geared up

The Henchman

for what I figured was going to be an extremely short murder session, or should I say suicide.

Then that Kinkaid boy grabbed me by the shirt collar and my arm cocked back and I was about to fire a right hook, when a loud "WHACK" resounded and down he went like a wet sack of corn meal. And then the next lad took a step closer, there was another loud "WHACK" and he too fell stretched out looking like a dead man. I know he looked like a dead man, for it was at the second loud "WHACK" that I'd opened up one of my tightly screwed shut eyelids. And there lay two bodies stretched out one atop the other as if they'd been gun shot and for the briefest of seconds I'd thought they had.

I was just unscrewing my other eye open and my jaw was on its way to the floor, when the third cowboy decided he didn't want to join the dog pile with his friends and made a hasty retreat, just not hasty enough. He had just executed as beautiful a pirouette as any ballerina, spun about face and was aimed the other way when another loud resounding "WHACK" thundered and he too went down, but he went down the steps and into the dirt face first. There was a loud burst of applause from the café as the crowd had watched those three cowboys corner me and witnessed them go down in defeat in three quick "WHACKS".

After the brief applause a loud voice beside me called out, "You rapscallions better git off my porch before you get another clout atop the head! And if'n you ever try and lay hands to my kin again, I'll put a hole in you, they can pass a canteen through without touching either side!" and with that Grumps waggled the cane he'd cracked them over the head with in one hand, and pulled his pistol from out of his overalls and fired a round into the crick off to one side.

I don't know if it had been the bucking horses or the "whack" on the heads that had sobered those drunks up, but if that didn't do it, that enormously loud pistol shot did. As if being raised from the dead, those three bodies quickly rose to their feet and ran off into the distance almost as fast as their horses had.

Archie Matthews

That pistol shot also had an instant effect on the café crowd, for just as quickly as they had piled outside to see the rodeo, they piled back in side as if set off on a foot race at the sound of the starting pistol. It always amazed me as a kid the kind of results Grumps could achieve by punctuating his sentences with a pistol shot. He could make people disappear quicker than any Magician could by waving a wand and shouting "Abaracadabara"!

The only bad thing about the whole thing was that pistol shot had also sounded all too familiar to both grandpa and grandma, who both had come hoofing it mighty quick from the house. I won't bore you with the details of who got chewed out about what, but there had been some mighty hard looks and a whole lot of accusations. But since nobody had actually seen "any going's on with the horses", there had only been some wild theories and accusing looks thrown my way, but I was smart enough to keep my mouth shut and let my shrugging shoulders do all the explaining.

It took grandpa the better part of the next day in questioning as many café patrons as he could find willing to talk, before he got a good gist of what had "Fired Grumps up enough to pull and shoot his old cap and ball revolver".

The best witness had been Grumps himself. For when grandpa put him to questioning, he said, "Me and my poor little great grandson was just a sit'n up here on my property enjoy'n a rodeo when we was up and attacked by three no accounts…..my porch was boarded and we set about to repel boarders to the best of our abilities." At this point he'd given me a sly wink. But since he'd lost me at the "repel boarders" part, all I could do was keep sitting quietly while Grump's head swiveled back to grandpa who was patiently sitting on the porch rail, listening intently, while grandma was standing tapping her toe with furrowed brow, her suspicious eyes swiveling from me to Grumps and back again.

The Henchman

"I will not stand by and allow my property to be boarded by a bunch of pirates, let alone stand and see my innocent great grandson butchered on my own porch. So's after we read em from the book about the error of their way, I sent em along at the point of my horse pistol….They was just lucky I didn't dust their britches with my shotgun and I only spooked em with my pistol…they come back here and attack a poor old man and his kin again, they are going to get a lot more than just a pistol shot in the air!" And with that, Grumps give a determined stubborn look and shook his crooked old willow cane, then thumped it point first into the porch. And that had ended that.

Nope, I knew I never had anything to fear from Grumps. Drunken cowboys and pirates better be scared to death of the old boy and his old cap and ball pistol, but not me his great grandson. As rough a customer as everyone said the old fellow had been and still was, to my reckoning, he'd never been anything but a kind and gentle great grandpa to me.

Thus seeing the store owner Ed Shotz headed back to open his store, and remembering I owed Grumps a lot more than just a soda, I ambled up the street towards the store.

Ed unlocked the door and took down the sign and was just about to shut the door again, when I stepped up and seeing me, he quickly opened the door wide.

"Hello there young man!" Ed grinned looking down at me.

I stepped inside and Ed shut the door and stepped around behind the counter and put on the big apron he always wore.

"And how may I help you sir?!" Ed smiled his eyes twinkling.

"Oh, Ed, I ain't a sir, I'm just a kid". I laughed, for he always made the same joke when I came to his store. He'd always call me "Sir" and make like I was some kind of rich grown up ready to spend a lot of money and I'd always remind him I was just a poor kid.

Archie Matthews

"Well, a kid can still be a sir.....so what'll it be? Do you need a new rifle to go bear hunting with? How about a couple of boxes of shells for hunting season? Maybe you need some chewing tobacco?" Ed asked with his teasing smile.

"Nope....Ed, you know I'm just a kid and can't bear hunt yet and I only chew gum not tobacco," I laughed and smiled like I always did when Ed teased me. "I'd like a bottle of soda pop", I smiled as innocently as I could.

Ed never missed a beat and still smiling said, "Oh, well ....you need a bottle of soda pop for old Grump?"

"No, Grump can't have soda, you know that. " I replied with as serious a look as I could muster.

"Well now, as long as it's for you and not for Grump.....do you want one of them bottles of Cola?" That tricky old store owner asked innocently. That crafty devil he knew I hated cola, while Grumps on the other hand, loved the stuff. It's mighty hard to keep a secret in a town as small as this one, and as Grumps had said, "Old Ed was bound to ask a lot of questions" and he did.

"Oh, no sir, you know I don't like Cola, I like that Lemon pop." I smiled as sweet and innocent as I imagined any soda loving angel ever did. I just kept imagining myself on a holy mission to get my dear old great grandpa a drop of pay back, after all, I was still remembering what he'd done for me away back when. The way I figured it, as long as I had a pure heart about the whole ordeal, I might just get away without being struck by lightning for my lies and deceit.

Grandma had drug me to the little white church at the far end of town more than once during my summer vacations with her and grandpa. I'd paid a bit of attention to the preacher in between my squirming and nodding off while he'd shouted about fire and brimstone and evil people being struck by lightning. Grandma was fond of reminding me, especially when she was suspicious

The Henchman

I'd done something but hadn't evidence enough for a conviction let alone a switching, saying "If'n you lie you can be struck by lightning."

Well I'd seen what happened to that Sexton boy that was struck by lightning, his hair turned white and his eyes all crazy and his taking off at a dead run every time a loud noise broke out. No sir, I didn't want any part of lightning, but I figured this as one of those "little white lies", I'd heard tell about and I figured as long as it was for a noble cause, I just might squeak by without being "Zapped" from above. And just like that, Ed gave me a smile, seeming to accept my bald face untruth for gospel. Thus, just as the Brooklyn Bridge exchanged hands during a shady business deal, so did a soda pop.

"Okay, one lemon pop coming up….that'll will be a dime." Ed said turning around and pulling open the old metal pop cooler lid and with a rustle of tinkling glass bottles, he pulled out a dripping wet bottle of "Mellow Yellow" soda pop. Putting the cap in the opener fastened to the cooler, he "Popped" the lid off and handed it to me. Then lay his hand out flat with the palm up and I placed the quarter Grumps had given me in it.

Ed looked at the quarter and suddenly gave a knowing smile and his eyes slid up from his hand and its telltale contents back to peer into my eyes. "Say now, that so happens to look like the very same quarter your Grumps took from me this morning….Your sure you're not buying this soda for him?"

And I'll be the first one to say, I felt a rush of static electricity tingling in my hair as if a bolt of lightning was taking deadly aim for the center of my noggin, but I managed to hold my composure. Even though it cost me a year or two right off the top of my maximum life expectancy for the fear of it.

"Well, the quarter "WAS" his, but he gave it to me, he said for me to spend it only here and make sure you seen it." I said, remembering what Grumps had said.

Archie Matthews

Ed suddenly laughed, so loud and sudden it almost scared the pants off me and I was sure he'd seen through the devious deception. "Well that's certainly Grumps for you, the old codger!" and then with a spin of the crank on the side of the old cash register and a "Ding" the drawer opened and he dropped the quarter inside and dug out a dime and a nickel and handed me the change.

With the hard earned nefarious bottle of soda in hand, I exited as quickly as I could and was running up the boardwalk and across the street to the grandparent's yard. Going through the gate, I quickly headed across the back yard headed for the far gate on the other side, but was suddenly stopped short as grandma came out the back porch door. I almost fell over faint, here I was "Ambushed" and caught red handed. I'd risked and narrowly avoided being struck and fried by a bolt of lightning, only to be taken captive and tortured by grandma and her nefarious willow switches.

"Where are you going with that soda?" grandma quickly asked shifting from her sweet loving grandma look into her evil inquisitor glare. My britches and backside literally heating up for the fear of the "Switching" that was about to come.

"I was going to go play down to the scrap yard….." I stammered.

"Where'd you get the money for that soda pop? Did Grumps give you money to go buy him a soda pop?" and her hot piercing eyes began to sear my flesh and I could have sworn I saw her willow switch 'n hand twitch. I could all but feel the thumb screws in place and tightening, but I knew if I spilled my guts now, I was a goner for sure, so I stuck with my story, and once again risked a fiery bolt from above.

"Grumps give me a quarter he won from Ed Shotz bet 'n Mr. Wellner would blow up the Café this morn'n, but this here is my pop, not his." I assured her and even took a long swig to seal the performance.

214

The Henchman

"Well you just see to it he don't wrestle it away from you….that old man would steal a pop from a kid if'n he could, to satisfy his craving for the sweets. You best just stay up here in the yard and drink your pop." And with a pat on the head she was off to the clothes line and I was suddenly sequestered and held prisoner in the yard. It would have been a death sentence for me to head out that gate now, what with the "Inquisitor and master torturer" having her suspicions raised, and I knew it.

I ambled around the yard and played up on the back porch and wandered around to the side yard and then up to the front porch. Once in a while I'd take a sip or two from the cool soda pop bottle, for being a kid is dry work and after all, it was summer. Besides, I knew good old Grumps would have shared a sip or two with me anyways. And as you might have guessed, as the heat of the afternoon had taken its toll, as did my being sequestered in the hot confines of the yard, before I knew it, the soda pop was gone and all I held was a dried out empty green pop bottle.

Lunch time came and went and although Grumps usually came up to the house and took meals with us he hadn't been up to it today, or so grandma had said. So after we had eaten our mid-day meal, grandma gave grandpa a small sack with Grumps lunch and asked him to deliver it.

Seeing my chance, to go visit Grumps and explain I had been watched to closely to deliver his soda, I quickly asked to go along with grandpa. "Okay, you can go along with me", grandpa said, "I'm headed up to Tick's to deliver their mail, you can ride along with me." And before I knew it, we were in the car and headed past the shop on our way out of town.

We stopped in front of Grumps cabin and grandpa left the car running as he stepped out and around and handed Grumps his sack lunch. Grumps was giving me the eyeball and all I could do was carefully and quickly show him the green soda pop bottle I still carried, but was now empty. I didn't realize it at the time, but Grumps old eyes couldn't distinguish that green bottle was empty, he just seen a soda bottle and I saw his eyes twinkle as he licked his lips.

Then grandpa turned and after giving Grumps an over the shoulder wave, he got back in the car and up the road we went to Uncle Tick and Aunt Edna's. As we drove off, I swiveled my head around and saw Grumps rocking in his chair so fast he seemed just a blur of motion as he worked up his thirst and anticipation for his soda pop.

I won't bore you with the long ride up the creek, over the old rickety bridge and across the creek to deliver the mail. I will say it was a long bumpy ride for a kid with a bladder stretched tight by a full bottle of pop. And as we pulled into Tick and Edna's, grandpa got out while I waited in the car. I couldn't get out for fear of trying to walk would set my drum tight bladder loose and I'd wet my pants. Therefore I did the only thing I could, and while grandpa was talking to Tick and Edna on their front porch, I quickly emptied my bladder in the only thing I had to hand, that empty green pop bottle.

I don't know why?!.....Who the heck can explain why kids do anything? As an adult now and after having kids myself, I now realize I could have very easily just opened the car door, stepped behind the car and "watered my mules". To this day, I don't know what possessed me to pee in that green pop bottle, but I did.

I will say, it was in the nick of time, for two reasons, my bladder had been stretched so big it felt like a Thanksgiving Day parade balloon and I no more than got my trousers fastened back up than back to the car grandpa came and we were off for home.

Again, I won't go into detail about the long boring drive back, other than to say it wasn't near as bumpy what with an empty bladder. But I will point out a startling fact, that after having drunk that bottle of pop, I'd evidently only stored up the liquid in my bladder, to end up returning nearly every drop back to the bottle, for it was as full as the moment it'd been opened. (Authors note, boys notice things like that…although I don't think girls even have a clue as to such things. After all, girls use "water closets" and wouldn't begin to know how to water a mule, let alone gauge input and out-take by careful bladder expansion calculations)

And then we entered town and Grumps seeing us, jumped up from his rocker and began jumping up and down, waggling his cane for us to stop. Which grandpa quickly did and rolling his window down he called out to Grumps, "What's up dad?"

"I need that boy to do some tote 'n and lift 'n for me" Grumps called back.

Grandpa turned around in his seat and began to say something, when suddenly he looked at the once again full soda pop bottle. "Say, I thought that bottle was empty when we left?" he said with a puzzled look.

"I had to pee….somewhere" I quickly explained.

"Well don't spill the dern thing in the car….go on and help Grumps then pour that out….and don't just throw the bottle down, put it out on the garbage heap!" and with that, grandpa leaned over and opened the care door and unknowingly sent me spiraling towards utter destruction, pop bottle and all.

I stepped out the car and as grandpa drove off, I began to formulate how I was going to explain to my dear old Grumps, how I'd drank his precious soda. I knew it wasn't going to be well received, so I was in no hurry as I trudged up the steps to Grumps. I had just gained the top of the steps and had opened my mouth and said, "Well Grumps, about the soda……" and held up the bottle, when vile treachery broke out, or at least from one old man's perspective.

Before I could say anymore or knew what was happening, Grumps quickly snatched the full green bottle from my hand and throwing it to his lips he took a hearty gulp. All I could do was

Archie Matthews

stand frozen in deep shock as suddenly the world shifted into slow motion.

I'll never forget the sparkle in that old man's eyes as his fingers grasped that green pop bottle and tipped it to his lips. I saw his child like grin of delicious expectation morph into pursing lips of anticipation as they fastened to the bottle opening. And before I could even formulate words of warning inside my head, let alone outside upon my lips, the deed was done.

At that precise moment I felt at least a year of my maximum life expectancy vanish in a quick invisible puff of smoke at the very realization of what had just happened, let alone what was about to come.

Who's to say if it went down his throat or his wind pipe, all I know is the old fellow got one single gulp started down when right back up it came with a loud snort of disgust. Grumps spit out what was left in his mouth and with the second ugliest look I've ever seen he said, shouted "That's the nastiest soda I ever tasted….tastes like ….." And then holding the bottle out and looking at it and then at me, his face suddenly screwed into the number one ugliest look I've ever seen.

"Thank God", that's when real time resumed, for if it hadn't, I'd have been a goner for sure, but as the mighty creator had seen fit to shift time back into high gear, so did my body as I ignited my booster rockets and kicked into hyper speed.

"WHY YOU LITTLE……." And with a "Swish" of his cane barely missing my noggin, I was off like a rifle shot……or should I say pistol shot, for as I picked my feet up and set them down for home, I kept expecting just that…..a resounding pistol shot from the old man, I'd just unwittingly poisoned.

I'm happy to report that pistol shot never sounded, although I don't know why, Grumps was certainly angry enough. The old fellow was so angry he wouldn't talk to me for almost a week, and every time I'd come to the shop and look his way, he'd give

The Henchman

me an evil eye that was fit to carve my gizzard and he'd shake his cane at me.

More than once or even twice he made evil motions across his throat with his finger and would then shake his fist at me. To say our friendship, let alone our relationship was a bit strained was to say the least. For when Grumps came to lunch or dinner, and someone would ask him why he seemed upset, he'd only say. "I was betrayed and set upon by my own Henchman and nearly poisoned to death! You'd be upset too if'n you had an evil henchman turn on you." And he'd give me such a despicable look I all but melted.

Although I and Grumps got a lot of puzzled looks from both grandma and grandpa, and there were questions thrown from every direction for many a year after that summer, I nor Grumps ever told anyone what happened.

That had been the summer Grumps had nicknamed me "The Henchman" and it stuck for as long as Grumps lived. It was "Grumps and his Henchman" from that day forward.

Oh, he finally forgave me, although I will say, he was forever wary and wouldn't accept a beverage from me, soda pop or not. And from that day forward much to everyone's surprise he would never accept a drink of anything without first seeing someone else take a sip first. Even before he'd take a sip of his morning coffee, he'd always wait and watch to see either grandma or grandpa sip theirs first.

I can't say I blame him one bit, for believe it or not, I am much the same. Life is funny how it teaches each of us the ups and the downs as we go through the years. I've learned in my lifetime not to up the bottom end of a soda pop or down the contents on a hot day, from the hands of a kid on a hot day……Henchman or otherwise.

Archie Matthews

THE END

The Henchman